Absence Management

'A Real World Approach'

by
Graham Smith

www.realworldapproach.com
realworldapproach@gmail.com

First Edition published in 2013

© Copyright 2013 Graham Smith

The right of Graham Smith to be identified as the author of this book has been asserted by him in accordance with the Copyright, Designs and Patents Act, 1988.

All rights reserved.

No part of this publication may be reproduced, stored in a retrieval system or transmitted in any form or by any means including photocopying, electronic, mechanical, photocopying, recording, scanning, or otherwise, without the prior consent of the copyright holder. Any unauthorised distribution or use of this text may be a direct infringement of the author's rights and those responsible may be liable in law accordingly.

To my partner Gill Donnell MBE for all her help and encouragement.

To my colleagues from Ashridge and the Chartered Institute of Personnel and Development, who have continually widened my horizons and challenged my thinking.

For Ben, Dan, Holly and Emily.

Index

Introduction: About this book   6

Chapter 1: Why focus on sickness absence   10

Chapter 2: The Investig8™ Model   16

Chapter 3: Initial Response   21
Phase 1: Initial Response
Real World Approach: Initial Response
Summary: Initial Response

Chapter 4: Collect Intelligence   33
Phase 2: Collect Intelligence
Real World Approach: Collect Intelligence
Summary: Collect Intelligence

Chapter 5: Plan   57
Phase 3: Plan
Real World Approach: Plan
Summary: Plan

Chapter 6: Gather Evidence   79
Phase 4: Gather Evidence
Real World Approach: Gather Evidence
Summary: Gather Evidence

Chapter 7: Develop Solution   97
Phase 5: Develop Solution
Real World Approach: Develop Solution
Summary: Develop Solution

Chapter 8: Implement   111

        Phase 6: Implement

        Real World Approach: Implement

        Summary: Implement

Chapter 9: Review   122

        Phase 7: Review

        Real World Approach: Review

        Summary: Review

Chapter 10: Protect   131

        Phase 8: Protect

        Real World Approach: Protect

        Summary: Protect

Chapter 11: Summary   146

INTRODUCTION: About this book

This book is aimed at all individuals and organisations that wish to improve their approach to absence management. It is not designed as a theoretical study purely of interest to the specialist; instead it offers practical insights, frameworks and tools that enable the reader to understand the true nature of absence and to confidently take the steps that are needed to achieve improvement for the benefit of all.

In an increasingly competitive and resource-constrained world, few would argue against the importance of taking every opportunity to improve productivity, customer service and financial performance. Despite this, it is rare to find an organisation that would claim it has done all it could to control and reduce the cost and negative service impact associated with sickness absence. Even in those organisations where management of individual cases is performed well, there is often limited appreciation of the wider strategic issues at play, thus reinforcing a perpetual reactive cycle, rather than stimulating the positive and proactive interventions that are needed if meaningful and sustained benefit are to be achieved.

The original inspiration for this book came from my time working alongside a number of highly dedicated and professional police officers and police staff. Seeing how those individuals approached some of the most complex and sensitive of issues, I was struck by their ability to take a seemingly indecipherable problem and reach a well thought out solution capable of standing up to the most rigorous of scrutiny. This caused me to question whether the same basic principles could be transferred to the world of work in a much broader sense.

In this book, you will be introduced to the Investig8™ model, a unique tool that takes the tried and tested principles used to solve serious crime and translates them to the world of work. The rigour that this framework offers enables you to gather the evidence necessary to construct a comprehensive picture of absence and thus be in a position to approach the matter strategically. In doing so, it also provides the necessary insights for the development of the bespoke solutions that will be required to address the unique circumstances that are relevant to your organisation.

If you are an HR Specialist, then following the Investig8™ approach will increase your credibility with operational colleagues and senior management. If you are a Chief Executive, Board Member or senior leader, the methodology that is promoted will provide you with the opportunity to improve both service delivery and your competitive position.

For the rest of us, this book provides a valuable insight into how as employees, managers, staff representatives, or as members of wider society we can all benefit from a more innovative and professional approach to the management of absence.

In writing this book I am conscious that whatever your organisational role, you are probably busier now than you have ever been. Therefore, no matter how well constructed the arguments may be or how effective the techniques are in their application, there is a danger that you may simply not have the time to finish this text and it could end up as shelf decoration, like many other management tomes before it. To avoid this potential pitfall, I have sought to recognise the differing needs and demands that you, the reader, are facing. For those who have the opportunity and require a detailed grasp of the concepts I would clearly encourage a cover-to-cover read. If, however, you have limited time and just need to understand the basic principles, each chapter contains a bullet point summary that will enable you to quickly gather an overall understanding; you can then dip in and out of the detail as required. Finally, I have also provided a 'real life' narrative within each chapter that takes the detailed theory and provides a simple demonstration of how the various techniques could be used in practice.

I hope you find the book enjoyable, beneficial and thought provoking but most of all a practical 'real world approach' to the problem of how to successfully manage absence. Should you wish to find out more about this topic, or some of the other 'real world' solutions that are available, please visit www.realworldapproach.com.

Chapter 1

Why focus on Absence?

Why focus on absence?

Before launching into the detail of how to deal effectively with absence management, it is worthwhile pausing to consider why it is such a key strategic issue for all organisations.

Given the wide-ranging demands of the modern world, it is hardly surprising to find that fundamentally improving absence doesn't always feature at the top of the organisational to-do lists; but it should. Absence from work has the potential to create significant additional costs and difficulties for organisations, which if not tackled effectively can prove fatal.

In addition to the obvious financial impact associated with factors such as occupational sick pay schemes and resourcing replacement staff, employers also face substantial direct and indirect costs as a result of impact on the wider business. Whilst customer service issues and reduced productivity are obvious side effects, the bad news doesn't stop there. The management costs resulting from the inevitable red tape and bureaucracy that are linked with managing absence, not to mention the personal impact on individuals and wider employee engagement, should not be under-estimated. Indeed there is a very real risk that individuals, teams and indeed whole organisations can find themselves falling into a negative culture of under-performance and apparent helplessness if sickness absence is not managed effectively.

Each year a number of well-respected surveys are carried out in an attempt to quantify the precise size of this problem. Almost inevitably there are variations in the figures quoted as a result of differences in source data. However, regardless of the starting point, the outcome invariably points to absence being a significant cost to organisations, individuals and wider society, which could and indeed should be reduced.

In the United Kingdom alone, the Office for National Statistics put the total amount of sickness absence for the country at 131 million days in 2011, representing an average of 4.5 days per employee. Whilst the most common reasons for absence were identified as minor illnesses such as coughs, colds and flu, the review concluded that the greatest number of days lost were for musculoskeletal problems, which accounted for more that a quarter of all sickness absence.

A year earlier, the Confederation of British Industry (CBI), working with Pfizer, put the figure for UK sickness at 190 million working days, creating an average of 6.5 days per employee at a direct cost to organisations of £17 billion. This was also estimated to include over £2.7 billion arising from 'non-genuine' sickness absence. While the CBI highlighted that some employers had been successful at bringing down levels of absence, their survey indicated that the gap between the best and worst performing organisations had widened and that the problem of 'non-genuine' sickness was on the increase. PwC, however, suggested that the overall size of the problem was far greater. In its 2010 survey, they point to the average number of unscheduled days absence in the United Kingdom being 10 days per employee, at a total cost to the economy of £32 billion, 80% of which directly related to sickness absence. According to the PwC survey, these figures were on par with much of Western Europe but around double that found in the United States and Asia.

Whilst all of the evidence points to wide variations in sickness rates across organisations, due to issues such as organisation size, sector of the economy, gender balance and age profile of the workforce, it is universally clear that opportunities to improve do exist. It is also commonly understood that effective processes for managing sickness absence are important, not only for organisations, but for wider society. The Centre for Economic and Business Research estimates that every year approximately 300,000 people in the UK leave employment because of illness or injury, often with significant impact on the individual and their family, as well as impacting on the country's health and benefit services.

For organisations the sums involved can be significant. In terms of estimated cost per employee, the CBI put the figures at £1,040 for each public sector employee and £710 per private sector employee, whilst Xpert HR quotes a more conservative average of £553 per employee. Whatever the true figure, the costs involved represent an organisational overhead that can in the majority of cases be much more effectively controlled. A failure to recognise this fact and not to focus on the issues adversely impacts not only on the financial bottom line, but also influences how its customers and indeed its own workforce view the organisation. Follow this to a logical conclusion and you end up with expensive public services and private sector organisations that are working to reduced margins, with customers, shareholder and staff who become increasingly dissatisfied with the situation.

Despite these significant issues, there are still many organisations that simply do not understand the full extent of the sickness absence issues they face. Whilst it is now unusual to come across a Chief Executive or HR Director who cannot immediately put their finger on the organisation's overall sickness rate, scratch beneath the surface and in many cases you will find an almost total lack of understanding of the bigger picture.

As competitive pressures continue to increase, the need to comprehensively address sickness absence and to understand the issues at play in your organisation and in wider society will intensify. It is no longer enough to simply know what the organisational sickness rate is and to have a policy for managing absence. Competitive advantage will only come from implementing a more comprehensive and integrated approach to the issue, an approach that can accommodate the many different facets involved, and bring them together in a flexible and yet systematic framework that can be easily understood by all.

In the chapters that follow, I will explain just how to implement such a methodology. For those that fully implement the approach detailed, I can promise a unique insight into the true nature of sickness absence as it impacts on your organisation and, as a result, provide the potential opportunity to develop a lasting solution to this fundamental issue.

CHAPTER 2

The Investig8™ Model

CHAPTER 2: The Investig8™ Model

The Invesitg8™ model is a unique management tool that takes the tried and tested investigative techniques that have been used successfully to solve serious crime over a number of years and converts them to the world of work. In doing so it provides a structured evidenced-based approach to problem solving. The resulting framework is not complicated to implement; as with all good models it is both simple and logical in its basic approach, but offers the prospect of real depth and insight.

Having worked closely with police officers and police staff over a number of years, I have seen at first hand their ability to respond quickly to any challenge, then systematically analyse the situation to arrive at a solution, often when faced with a seemingly impossible problem. The automatic response when presented with this impressive skill set is to put it down to their extensive and detailed training in how to solve crime. Over time, however, I began to wonder whether the basic principles that these individuals were using so successfully, could form the basis for dealing with wider organisational issues. It was from this point that I started to research the exact nature of the processes involved and to work out whether those processes were transferable.

Being in the fortunate position of having a number of experienced ex-officers as close personal friends, I shamelessly imposed on their goodwill and spent many a weekend talking to them about how they had approached the range of serious incidents that had shaped their careers. It became perfectly clear, in the course of those discussions, that there was a basic underlying approach to police investigations that had wider business application. It was from this that the Invesitg8™ model was born; a straightforward and logical process that can be used by any business to tackle an almost limitless array of issues. Whilst the model has its origins firmly based in professional police investigative practices, what is presented here is a refined and simplified version of those practices that offers much wider relevance and greater transferability.

The model itself consists of eight distinct phases, namely:

1. Initial Response

Assess the situation and take any immediate steps that are required.

2. Collect Intelligence

Obtain the background intelligence needed to gain a more informed understanding of the situation.

3. Plan

Review the intelligence, develop hypotheses and plan the evidence gathering.

4. Gather Evidence

Seek the evidence to prove or disprove the hypotheses.

5. Develop Solution

Use the evidence to develop the correct solution.

6. Implement

Takes steps to ensure the effective implementation of the solution.

7. Review

Check that the solution has worked as intended.

8. Protect

Learn the lessons and continue to develop.

You can use the Investig8™ model organisation-wide or in a specific business area; importantly it does not need a 'crisis' in order to offer substantial benefit. For the purposes of this book we will be focusing specifically on how Investig8™ can enable you to better understand and manage absence in order to create competitive advantage, but its application is far wider than that. As a model, Investig8™ can be used to assist any organisation, from any sector, in a multitude of different ways, including new product development, change management and general performance improvement. The insights provided by following each part of the process will help you to better understand the key issues facing your business and appreciate what actions are required to obtain sustained improvement. Used correctly, Investig8™ moves organisations away from ill thought out, costly and poorly researched 'silver bullet' solutions, to proper evidence based outcomes that will stand up to scrutiny. It also overcomes the argument that proper investigation takes too long or is too complicated, providing as it does a truly proportionate approach to establishing the facts relevant to the 'case' and developing solutions based on those facts.

In the remaining chapters of this book, I will take you through each phase of the process in turn. For those that do not have the time to read the entire content, I have provided a bullet point summary for each chapter; this will enable you to quickly gather an understanding of the Investig8™ model. I have also provided 'real life' narrative within each chapter that takes the detailed theory associated with each phase and provides a simple demonstration of how the various techniques can be used in practice.

CHAPTER 3

Initial Response

Phase 1: Initial Response

An organisation can identify a sickness absence problem by any number of different means. Normal monitoring arrangements may highlight a worsening trend, operational managers may identify difficulties due to the absence of key staff, or there may simply be organisational pressure to bring costs under control. Regardless of how it is initially identified as an issue, the outcome is almost inevitably the same. Everyone wants to see the rate of absence reduced and reduced quickly. The reason for this reaction is obvious. Absence is seen as something that organisations can control, even if they cannot totally eradicate it. Once a problem has been surfaced 'do nothing' is, therefore, not an option and as any delay is seen as potentially harmful, the overwhelming desire will be to implement a swift solution.

The Invesitg8™ model recognises this need for immediate action through 'INITIAL RESPONSE', but in doing so it also ensures that it is highlighted as the first phase in a wider, more structured solution that offers greater surety of long-term benefits. Fundamentally, there is nothing wrong with a rapid response, as it can provide a sense of urgency and if correctly targeted can produce quick wins that encourage the organisation to seek further gains. The trick, however, is to identify what should be tackled immediately and what requires a more in-depth investigation of the issues before a solution is developed.

The first element of the 'INITIAL RESPONSE' phase in a police investigation is to establish just who the 'victim' is and to get a clear account from them of the key issues. For our purposes, the 'victim' equates to the 'client' you are working for. In many cases, this will be the Chief Executive or other member of the senior executive team, but the client could be your immediate boss, an HR specialist, a functional manager, or a myriad of other individuals. Ultimately, what is important is not who the client is or the precise detail of that relationship, but making sure that the correct client has been identified and that you have a clear understanding of what they perceive the problem to be.

At this phase of the overall process, the requirement is to be in full 'receive' mode, listening to points being raised and teasing out further detail. This is not the time to be on 'transmit', giving your opinion as to what the issues might be. The key fact to remember is that you are not aiming to provide the ultimate solution, so there is no need to judge, defend or proffer an alternative view. What is required is a full understanding of what the client perceives as the true nature of the problem; this helps with identifying some initial lines of enquiry and will allow you to pinpoint who some of the significant 'witnesses' may be. Whether the client's initial assessment is ultimately proved right or wrong is something that will come out later as part of the overall Investig8™ process.

Those who have ever been involved in any form of investigative process will know that whilst it sounds easy, obtaining a clear and meaningful statement is an art. You need to know when to prompt, when to stay silent and when to probe further. If you are able to access a trained and experienced investigator at this stage of the process, it will offer the opportunity to maximise potential benefits in the longer term. Otherwise, plan your client meeting carefully to ensure that you tease out all of the available information.

Once you have a suitable statement, the second element of 'INITIAL RESPONSE' is the completion of a provisional risk assessment. It is important not to get lost in the detail at this point and to focus on the word 'provisional'. Do not get distracted by a long list of potential risks, this is not the point. We will review all of the main threats and risks as part of Phase 2 - 'COLLECT INTELLIGENCE'. The only threats and risks you should aim to tackle during 'INITIAL RESPONSE' are those that are so significant and the cause so evident that immediate action is required. For example, faced with significant numbers of people with long-term back injuries, taking the immediate step of introducing or refreshing manual handling training may represent a justifiable initial response. Whether dealing with back injuries alone will ultimately solve a wider absence problem will need further investigation, but removing at least one obvious 'smoking gun' certainly makes the world a safer place and benefits both staff and the organisation.

In summary, 'INITIAL RESPONSE' is an important part of the overall process. If done properly, it provides the opportunity to gain a clear understanding of who the client is, what they see as the problem, who may be a useful 'witness' and where to start looking. Furthermore, it ensures that the organisation receives immediate protection from the most significant threats and risks. It can also demonstrate a definite intent to deliver, as well as providing quick wins to give momentum to the wider investigation.

'Real World Approach' – Initial Response

Anywhere Inc. is a multi-site manufacturing organisation, operating in a highly cost sensitive market. For some time, management had identified effective sickness management as a mechanism for controlling costs. Over the last 12 months absence rates had, however, been on the increase and the Chief Executive was now calling for immediate action to address the problem.

As Chief Executives go Helen Starling was reasonable and fair, but sickness issues were beginning to try her patience. 'We appear to have yet another issue with sickness management. It is only a couple of years ago that I needed to step in personally to address a problem with one of our factories, but here we are again talking about absence and this time we are looking at an upward trend across the organisation that shows no sign of abating.'

Marcus Denning was the new HR Director, a recent appointment for Anywhere Inc. and the latest addition to the Board. Keen to make a good impression for his new boss during his first Board meeting Marcus jumped straight in. 'I'll take that on and have a quick look to see what the issues are. I should be able to get an initial improvement plan drafted over the next week or so.'

Helen appeared suitably grateful. 'Thanks Marcus, it would be good to finally get somewhere with this and make a lasting improvement. As I said, this isn't the first time we have had this problem so something clearly needs to change.'

Returning to his office, Marcus cleared part of the email backlog and placed a call to his Senior HR Business Partner to see what information was available on sickness so that he could begin to identify the issues. Recognising the importance of getting the Chief Executive on-side right from the start, Marcus also took the precaution of booking a slot in her diary to make sure he understood exactly what, if any, perceptions she may already have about the nature of the sickness absence problem in the organisation.

It didn't take long for the Business Partner to arrive. For Marcus, Bob Ainsworth was worth his weight in gold, he had been around the organisation for years and was a constant source of valuable information.

'Just finished your first meeting with the Chief Executive then?'

'Yes; and I've picked up a little task, but it shouldn't be too much trouble. The Board is concerned about sickness rates rising over the last 12 months and want to find out what's going on as the extra costs are having an impact on profitability. I've booked in with the Chief Executive to make sure I get a proper understanding of what she thinks the problem is. She is the client for this piece of work, but I'd welcome your take on it as well. Are you aware of any major threats or risks that play into this issue that we should take some immediate action to contain?'

Bob Ainsworth had been here before and he pointed out that sickness was a perennial issue. 'We've had initiatives in the past to tackle various sickness related issues, but it always ends up coming back as a problem. It's easy to say you want to reduce it, but actually getting a reduction and making it stick is something of a holy grail around here. Anyway, I'll send over a copy of the latest data as soon as I get back to my desk and you can see for yourself.'

As soon as the data arrived, Marcus started sifting through the mass of figures in an attempt to identify the key threats and risks, but it was not going to be easy. There was sickness summary data for each Department and a region-by-region breakdown, but that was about as far as it went. The bundle of data that sat behind the summary information was extensive, albeit it was hard to navigate and make out anything meaningful without a lot of effort. Settling in for a late night, he began to wish he'd been a little bit slower in volunteering to sort it out.

The next day Marcus called in bright and early for his appointment with the Chief Executive.

'I see you were burning the midnight oil last night. Find anything useful?'

Not wanting to appear anything other than an insightful guru in front of his new boss, Marcus leapt in. 'It's not been easy with the way the data is formatted, but I can already see that stress related absence is a key risk. I'm thinking of arranging a trial for a workplace counselling service, with the aim of getting them to focus on the long term cases that are clearly hitting our figures.'

'Sounds good. So what do you want from me?'

'I'd be interested in your take on the problem. I always try to approach these things by thinking of it in terms of a client/contractor relationship. As you're my client, it's important that I fully understand the issue from your perspective, then I can work with you to find a solution.'

'That's easy, I just want sickness rates reduced once and for all,' replied the Chief Executive. 'Have you any idea how much it cost us last year in terms of sick pay, overtime and temps, not to mention lost productivity?'

Marcus got a sudden sinking feeling. The Chief Executive seemed far from engaged in the idea of clarifying things, but he decided to push the point a little further. 'I do appreciate what you are saying and clearly that is what I will aim to deliver; however, if you have any views on what has caused the problem, it would help to understand them so I know that I've specifically addressed those issues as part of the solution.'

Helen sat and thought for a moment. 'In reality it's difficult to say. I get to see a quarterly summary sheet of sickness and that clearly shows we have been on an upward trend, which been quite marked over the last 12 months. Apart from that, as Chief Executive I don't get to see the detail, there's so much to do that I can't spend my time digging to identify the root causes of everything. What I do know is one of our factories had a dramatic fall in productivity a couple of years ago and when I did look into that particular issue I found they had a problem with back injuries. I stepped in, made it clear that I needed things to be addressed and we got that sorted. It might be that same issue has cropped up again, but I'm sure you'll get to the bottom of it. Anything else?'

Marcus took the hint and headed for the door. It was time to go over the initial information he'd gathered and identify the key threats and risks that needed immediate attention.

At the following week's Board meeting Marcus announced that whilst he had still to complete the full review, he felt it was necessary to take some immediate steps to contain a couple of key risks. He highlighted that he had taken the precaution of implementing a trial of workplace counselling to address the problem of long term stress related absence and also announced that he'd commissioned some manual handling training to contain the potential threat posed by back injuries hitting production, as it had done in the past.

Everyone was suitably impressed. The Chief Executive made encouraging noises about decisive action being taken and that Marcus had been a good appointment. Even the Finance Director was on board, pointing out the significant invest-to-save advantages that could come from the two initiatives that were being implemented.

It was a good starter for ten; Marcus had the support of the Board and now he had the time to take a proper look at the problem by gathering the intelligence that would provide a comprehensive background.

Summary - Initial Response

1. Establish who the 'client' is.

2. Get a full statement from the 'client' so you understand the 'key issues' as they perceive them.

3. Carry out a provisional assessment of risk.

4. Take immediate steps to contain any key threats and risks.

CHAPTER 4

Collect Intelligence

Phase 2: Collect Intelligence

For many organisations 'INITAL RESPONSE' is as far as they get. This is an entirely understandable, if unfortunate, position. Nobody, faced with a problem, wants to spend any more time than necessary seeking a solution. If you have taken action quickly to deal with the most obvious risks and the problem appears to dissipate then it shows you were right and your years of managerial experience have once more demonstrated your judgment is sound, so why look any further? In reality, it is highly likely that all you have done is apply a sticking plaster to the problem or simply deflected it elsewhere. If you are lucky and the issue isn't too serious then this may be sufficient, at least in the short-term. However, if there are wider complications, treating the immediate symptoms will not bring the organisation back to full health; at best it will be a short-term recovery and you will be left with a perpetual reactive cycle.

If you are going to deal effectively with an absence management problem, then you must develop a full understanding of the context and this requires you to 'COLLECT INTELLIGENCE'. A fundamental part of the overall Investig8™ process is, therefore, to collect a comprehensive range of background intelligence before moving on to 'PLAN' the investigation. A failure to take this step is likely to lead to an unstructured and undirected approach to the problem, which can eventually result in the organisation investing time and money into sub-optimal or entirely inappropriate solutions.

'COLLECT INTELLIGENCE' starts by pulling together a wide range of potentially useful information. Not all of that information will ultimately go on to become intelligence; some will just be 'noise' that could potentially get in the way and slow the process of developing understanding of the issue at hand. For example, in conducting an environmental scan, we might establish that a competitor has recently opened a new outlet. Whilst this is potentially useful information for the organisation, it is unlikely to provide any useful intelligence as to why sickness has increased over the last 12 months. The aim, therefore, is to sift through the data, disregard the 'noise' and focus on the key pieces of intelligence that offers the potential of useful insight.

In terms of where to look, the Investig8™ model allows you to 'COLLECT INTELLIGENCE' from any number of sources. Remember, at this stage in the process we are not just looking for hard data, but also the opinions and views of individuals. We need not limit ourselves to pure fact this early on in the process; that is for the evidence-gathering phase, which comes later. For now we can feel free to spread the net far and wide.

Examples of potential sources of intelligence include:

Performance Data;

Environmental Scans;

Threat and Risk Assessments;

Results of Past Audits;

Organisational stories;

Customer reviews and articles;

Interviews with individuals;

Input from Specialists.

Whilst it would be difficult to find many who would argue against the benefits of collecting intelligence from all of these sources, in practice this is seldom done. As a result, organisations tend to operate absence management practices with a surprising lack of understanding about what is actually going on. If you don't believe me ask the following questions in your own organisation and see what response you get:

What does the performance data on sickness show as the top three factors impacting on absence levels?

Does the environmental scan show up any interesting case law or 'best practice' developments related to absence management that we need to consider further?

What is the greatest potential risk we face in terms of our ongoing management of absence?

Have we ever done a proper audit of our sickness management processes? If we did what were the findings, were they implemented fully and what impact did they have?

Are there any organisational stories circulating in relation to sickness absence?

What do first-line managers and trade union representatives think about the organisations approach to the management of absence?

Who has the worst sickness record in the organisation? How is this case being managed?

What advice have we received from our occupational health specialist in relation to our current profile of absence?

Faced with these questions, none of which are unreasonable, the traditional response of many is to bluster, state that the answer to these queries are obvious or give some vague reply. If that is the response you get, just push back a little and ask to see the evidence that supports what you are being told. You may be surprised by what you find and how thin the intelligence base is to justify the organisations current improvement plan for sickness ... assuming one even exists.

The other common response is ... 'We simply do not have the time or resources to look at this problem in that much detail, it is just one of a hundred things we need to do'. My response to this is to ask how much absence management currently costs the organisation. If you are a kind soul then simply ask for this in terms of direct costs, if you are feeling more challenging then ask them to factor into their financial estimate how much this equates to in terms of lower customer satisfaction and sales. Armed with this information you can then get those same individuals to do a brief comparison against the investment they are making in other projects and the answer should become obvious. In reality, 'COLLECT INTELLIGENCE' isn't difficult and it isn't costly or time consuming, it can just appear that way to the uninitiated.

In an effort to convince you of just how important and beneficial it is to have access to good intelligence I have set out below details of some of the sources that can be used and an indication of the potential valuable insight they can provide.

Performance Data

Performance data is perhaps the most obvious and most prevalent form of background intelligence. It is rare today not to find an organisation that is collecting data about sickness type, frequency, duration, etc. and then mapping this against a variety of workforce information such as age, gender, work type, location. Interestingly, the issue for most is, therefore, not a lack of such data but establishing a mechanism that allows you to identify and focus on what the most important aspects of the data are, so you can quickly recognise positive and negative trends.

Ultimately, the range of data you gather needs to be decided by the organisation, there is no 'one size fits all'. Whilst there are some general factors that always warrant attention such as age and gender, others will be industry specific and might relate to factors such as the nature of shift work, workplace, job type, salary grade, etc. Other factors may change over time, for example, it might be particularly critical to look in detail at the sickness of staff working on the development of a particularly important product, but once that item is in production the focus may change to the sales force.

The solution is to make sure that you implement a reporting mechanism for your data that is simple and flexible, provides easy focus on the most important issues and quickly identifies trends. It doesn't matter what format the data takes, as long as it is providing you with useful intelligence that can help to inform your decision-making.

Environmental Scan

Organisations often carry out quite sophisticated scans of their environment in an attempt to gain a level of foresight as to the key issues that will impact on the organisation and thus gain some form of competitive advantage. Common approaches that are used include detailed analysis of a particular industry or competitor, an assessment of the organisations strengths, weaknesses, opportunities and threats (SWOT analysis) or a PESTEL analysis, which look at the environment in terms of political, economic, social, technological, environmental and legal factors.

Carrying out a specific environmental scan for absence management offers the opportunity to gain valuable insights and, as a result, competitive advantage from a better understanding of issues relevant to sickness. If we rely, as many do, solely on internal performance data, we have no indication of context or of what might hit us in the future, thus we miss out on valuable information that could inform our approach. For example, stress may be a major factor behind sickness absence in the organisation, but how do we stand against others in the same sector, what is the national trend, what case law and best practice exists, what initiatives are government promoting? These and other similar questions all go unanswered if we do not carry out an effective environmental scan.

What form the environmental scan takes and how in-depth you opt to go are matters of choice for the organisation, but as a minimum I would recommend that you use the scan to identify:

Comparative data;

National trends in absence;

New developments and 'best practice';

Case law and legislation.

You can identify all of this information for yourself, as it is readily available in various reports, professional journals, newspaper articles and Internet sources. Alternatively, there are specialist companies available that will carry out dedicated environmental scans for you or provide access to generic scanning material covering this subject area.

Assessment of threat and risk

Whilst risk assessments are a common feature in many organisations, they tend not to be used as an intelligence tool for dealing with specific problems such as absence management. At best, sickness may feature as a single risk in an overall organisational risk assessment but this underplays its significance to the organisation, both in terms of cost and reputation. Furthermore, this approach ignores the intelligence opportunity that is offered by considering the matter in greater detail.

Remember, as part of 'INITIAL RESPONSE', we have already carried out a provisional assessment of risk, but now we are looking to establish a more comprehensive view of the threats and risks that exist. The outcomes from this process can then help to shape the 'PLAN' for the investigation and this in turn will lead to the further identification or reassessment of risks as part of developing our eventual solution.

In terms of process to follow, there are many different methodologies that exist for the assessment of threat and risk, but in essence they all attempt to identify:

> *What are the main threats/risks that we face?*
>
> *If the threat or risk became a reality, how impactive would it be?*
>
> *How likely is it to happen?*
>
> *What can be done to minimise the exposure?*

The assessment process itself can be carried out by an individual or by a team; it can also be done by internal staff or external consultants. Remember, this is not an exact science; ultimately, the likelihood of a particular outcome is a judgment call, albeit a judgment call based upon a structured assessment of risk, not merely a 'gut reaction'.

One of the reasons why organisations often fail to carry out a proper threat and risk assessment for issues such as sickness management, is that the assessment process itself can be perceived as overly cumbersome. In reality, this potential problem can be easily avoided, provided the scope of the risk assessment is limited to the key issues associated with the matter at hand. If you fail to take this step, it is easy to become distracted and extend the assessment to cover a wide variety of organisational issues that are not directly connected to the current issue, or go into too much detail around a specific point and, as a result, you lose direction. One tip is to use a simple scoring system based on factors such as the likelihood of the risk becoming a reality and the severity of the impact it would have; then make sure that you only focus on risks above a certain minimum score. This approach will ensure that you are only looking at the risks most likely to happen and have the most impact, thus reducing the number of items to be considered and making the whole process easier to manage.

Audits

Reviewing information from past audits can prove a very useful source of background intelligence. If sufficiently thorough, an audit can point to areas of strength as well as areas of weakness that will help to inform your thought processes as you move on to 'PLAN' the investigation.

It is not unusual to find that a past audit has highlighted particular vulnerabilities, which at the time were not viewed as critical and as a result were never addressed. What better place to start looking than the place where previous strengths and weaknesses were identified after a detailed review.

If an audit has never been conducted, then you may wish to take the opportunity to conduct an appropriate assessment. Remember, however, that the audit in itself will not provide the solution; it will only provide background intelligence that will help inform your thinking.

Organisational Stories, Customer Reviews, Articles, Interviews with Individuals, Input from Specialists

Whilst not always used, audits, risk assessments, data analysis and environmental scans tend to be readily accepted by organisations as they are viewed as providing 'hard' evidence.

The same cannot be said, however, of intelligence that is provided from organisational stories, customer reviews, articles, interviews and inputs from specialists. The qualitative information that these sources provide does, however, offer another type of insight that will never be obtained on the basis of facts and figures alone and should not be underestimated.

Whilst some of the information obtained might be mere opinion and have no basis in fact, it should not simply be disregarded. In one organisation I visited there was a significant amount of attention being paid to customer satisfaction. Information was regularly obtained against a variety of different factors that were felt to impact on satisfaction rates, one of which was speed of contact. Despite increased investment, anticipated improvements in performance had yet to materialise and the organisation was focused on finding even more resource, whilst simultaneously seeking to reduce customer demand. The organisational story that was circulating, however, was of an absence problem within that team and a subsequent review of the data found a sickness rate that was twice the organisational average. Without paying attention to the 'soft' data this fact may never have surfaced, as the relevant piece of 'hard' information was hidden by the reporting mechanism for absence, which was focused at departmental rather than team level.

Stories such as these are not unusual. Corridor talk, unofficial views of staff representatives, organisational myths and legends all provide useful background information that may offer valuable intelligence. Even when that intelligence differs across various parts of the organisation, it can offer useful insight. One team may have a view that poor attendance is never challenged and another could highlight examples of staff being too harshly dealt with; ultimately, both these views are valuable as part of establishing the overall picture.

Having hopefully persuaded you that gathering a wide range of information from a variety of sources is beneficial, the next requirement, as we've already touched on, is to sift that data and remove the 'noise' so that we are only left with useful intelligence. In reality, there is a need for an element of professional judgment in making this assessment, as you should ensure that you are removing that which is irrelevant, untrusted or of dubious quality, whilst retaining the challenging and uncomfortable, provided it is appropriately focused and adding value. Although it would be nice to build up a scientific basis for what to include and what to ignore, the reality is that such a process would overly complicate matters and be of limited value. Remember, at this stage we are simply establishing the background that will help us to 'PLAN' the investigation. What we are not doing is presenting this intelligence as fact on which to build an eventual solution. That said, we clearly want to have as much confidence as possible that the intelligence we have is accurate, as this will enable us to confidently move forward. If we are to achieve this, it is necessary to spend some time validating the intelligence we intend to rely upon.

Validation can take many different forms. For example, you could use techniques such as triangulation to validate the accuracy of specific items of data, or look to factors such as previous history to validate the source of a piece of information. Whatever the nature of the validation process, the aim is the same; to build confidence in the accuracy of the intelligence we will be using to help 'PLAN' the investigation.

One final point to highlight is that new intelligence will continue to come forward as the investigation progresses. That new intelligence should always be considered, no matter how late in the day, as it could offer a piece of 'killer' insight. This means that you may find yourself revisiting this phase on more than one occasion and altering your 'PLAN' to ensure that the evidence you go on to gather and the solution you eventually create is built upon the best possible information.

'Real World Approach' - Collect Intelligence

Back in his office, the HR Director made the obligatory phone call to his Senior HR Business Partner. 'Bob, can you get me the sickness summary data for the last 5 years, I want to take a look at trends for each Department and each region over a longer period of time. I'd also like some additional background intelligence collecting; carry out an environmental scan for me, you know one of those PESTEL things. See if you can find any national reports, survey data, examples of best practice, that sort of stuff, so I can put something meaningful and in-depth to the Board.'

Safe in the knowledge that a mass of information was now on its way, Marcus set off to deal with the disciplinary hearing he was due to Chair. He hated this aspect of the job, half the time you were dealing with stuff that wouldn't have been an issue if the local line manager had just dealt with it at an early stage; instead, problems are left to fester and HR have to pick up the pieces.

Three hours later, Marcus hadn't changed his view; another dismissal that wouldn't have arisen if the relevant manager had just dealt with the early warning signs. Wandering back to the office he bumped into the union representative who had been presenting the case for the defence.

'That was a total disgrace!' said Shelly

'Oh come on we can't have people falsifying time-sheets, it's no different to sticking your hand in the till.'

'Maybe, but it's one rule for one and one rule for another. That line manager is just a bully. If you're in with him you're okay, he'll cover for you, let you go early, even put you down as being at work when you are off sick; but if you're not part of his crowd there's no slack at all.'

'Come on it can't be as bad as all that.'

'Oh yes it can, it happens right across the Operations Division, bunch of alpha males if you ask me, normal rules don't seem to apply to them.'

Marcus carried on towards his office but then decided to take a little detour. It was time to spend a few hours 'walking the floor' to see if there was any more useful intelligence that he could pick up on the culture of the place.

A couple of days later Bob Ainsworth called in to see Marcus and handed over the information he had gathered. 'There's quite a lot of stuff here. It took me ages to work out how to sort out that environmental scanning bit, but once I got the hang of it I was able to pull it all together without too much trouble.'

'Bob, do you think we have a problem with under-recording of sickness absence.'

'I'm sure there's some, there always is, but as for how much of a problem it is I wouldn't like to hazard a guess.'

'Well I've been having a bit of a wander round and I had a chat to a few different managers and supervisors; very enlightening. Most wouldn't say anything, probably too worried they'd get into trouble, but one or two did let on that under-recording is an issue in Operations. Looks like they've got their favourites and been playing "Mr. Nice Guy" by putting people down as being at work when in fact they are tucked up under the duvet.'

'So do you still want all of this stuff?' said a rather despondent looking Bob. 'It would be a shame to throw it all away now; we don't normally get to look into things in any depth. In the past we've dealt with one-off issues, like that time when the Chief Executive went mad about sickness in that factory. We put in place interventions that seemed very successful at the time, but they didn't have any research behind them; this is different. There's some really good material here showing best practice from other organisations and lots of national reports that make interesting reading as well. If I'm honest I was a bit taken aback when I found out what the true cost of sickness is estimated to be across our industry; no wonder the Board want it investigated.'

'I'll take a proper look at it Bob don't worry, I'm sure there are a few golden nuggets in here, but if we haven't got complete records, we won't know what solutions we need to implement. It's probably that which has contributed to the short-lived nature of the benefits from previous initiatives.'

As Bob headed off Marcus began to pore over the organisational sickness data that he had dropped off. It was clear when you looked at the summary data over the last 5 years that this problem had been slowly building for some time, but nobody had really noticed what had been happening and he could understand why. In reality there was too much data to digest, too much detail, making it difficult to spot the trends and see what was going on. He made a mental note that this was something that needed to be addressed for the future.

Turning to the information that had been gathered as part of the environmental scan, Marcus could see that it had thrown up some interesting facts. Bob had done a good job on trawling through websites and journals to pick up examples of what others were doing. There were a couple of extensive government-sponsored reports that served to demonstrate that sickness was a big issue for lots of companies, not just for Anywhere Inc.; at least that was some small comfort. However, the comparative data Bob had picked up from other organisations and from industry surveys didn't make for good reading. Overall sickness rates for the organisation were just above the sector average, but the killer issue was the immediate competition who were reporting much lower rates of absenteeism; perhaps that was one of the reasons why they always seemed to be ahead and were top of the customer satisfaction league tables.

It was time to start collating all of this information and getting the organisation to focus on what needed to be done. That meant sifting through all of the material that had been gathered and separating out the 'noise' from the genuine pieces of intelligence. Marcus was already convinced that the big issue was under-reporting of sickness. It wouldn't be a popular message, but if the data wasn't complete then any improvement plan created was just based on guesswork. Thinking it through he decided to start by preparing a detailed assessment of the threats and risks associated with the organisation's current sickness issues so he could use that as a key focal point when developing the report.

The rest of the week was something of a blur. The disciplinary case that he'd just finished came back onto his desk in the form of an appeal and there had been some trouble over in Sales regarding new mileage rates and limits that had been put in place for expense claims. The report for the Board was going to have to wait.

The next meeting came around and Marcus set out where he'd got to. 'We don't have a full report for today's meeting as we are still investigating, but I can give a verbal update on the background intelligence I've collected so far. This matrix that I'm handing around the table sets out the main threats and risks as I currently see them.'

Joe Shiner, the Operations Director was first to speak up. 'This matrix is a bit busy isn't it? What are all of these colours and scores?'

'The key is there at the bottom of the page Joe; essentially, I've looked at the range of risks and scored them on the basis of how likely they are to happen and how much of a problem they would be if they did actually occur. Depending on the score I've then colour-coded them red, amber or green so we can quickly see what we should be focused on.'

'So what's this red risk at the top of the page then about

53

under-reporting of sickness and the reference to Operations'

'I was going to come on to that; whilst it's just background intelligence at the moment, I think we've got a big problem. I've talked to a few people now who point to a culture of under-reporting sickness. The only examples I've had quoted at the moment are from Operations, but I need to investigate further before I can be certain of how far this might go. The big issue is that if this turns out to be correct our data is incomplete so we can't rely on any solutions we put in place being the right ones, that's why it's got such a high score.'

Joe was starting to go a nice shade of purple. 'Are you trying to say that the biggest problem we have with sickness is that my staff aren't recording it? I think you should look closer to home before you start insinuating things like that. Everyone knows that it's the support service functions that are the real problem in terms of sickness. The only reason they haven't been tackled is because the rest of us are grateful they're not around to get in the way of the people doing the real work.'

Marcus was boiling inside, but he knew he didn't have all the information he needed yet to prove what the problem was. His gut reaction was Operations were a big problem, that was why Joe was being so aggressive, but without a proper investigation he couldn't prove it.

'I'm starting to sense a little tension in the air' said the Chief Executive. 'Shall we calm it down a bit. What is it you would like us to agree to Marcus?'

'As I was attempting to point out earlier, at the moment all I've got is some background intelligence that points towards the existence of a number of problems and under-reporting appears to be one of them. What I need now is a bit of time and resource to investigate fully so I can evidence things one way or the other. At our last meeting I put in a couple of early initiatives that were aimed at minimising some of the key risks and I'm happy that they are working and we now have a bit of time to tackle this problem properly.'

The Chief Executive summed up. 'Well we all heard about the potential invest to save benefits of dealing with this at our last meeting, so stay behind and we'll have a chat about how we set that up. Anybody disagree? Joe anything to add? Okay people lets call it a day and get out there to do some real work.'

As everyone left the room, Marcus gathered the copies of the risk matrix together and waited for the Chief Executive to start the discussion.

Summary – Collect Intelligence

1. Don't stop at the initial response.

2. Collect intelligence to help establish the background and thus assist the planning of the investigation.

3. Review the organisation's absence management data and identify possible key issues and trends.

4. Carry out an environmental scan.

5. Carry out an assessment of threat and risk.

6. Collect intelligence from organisational stories, reviews, articles, interviews and specialist input.

7. Sift the information to establish what is intelligence and what is simply 'noise'.

8. Collate and validate the intelligence.

CHAPTER 5

Plan

Phase 3: Plan

Having 'COLLECTED INTELLIGENCE', the next phase of the process is to 'PLAN' the investigation. Whilst a single individual could do this, the Investig8™ model recognises the added benefit that can be obtained from involving a range of people with different skill sets and different opinion and recommends the creation of a 'Gold Group'.

The 'Gold Group' is regularly used in policing to deal with critical incidents and operates at a strategic level. The Group is formed by bringing together all of the key players essential to identifying a solution. These key players can come from any part of the organisation and from any position. Levels of seniority are not important; what is important is the individual's ability to play a positive role in finding a solution.

The purpose of the 'Gold Group' is to review the intelligence that has been collected so far and to take a strategic view of the issues in order to 'PLAN' the investigation. When deciding who to involve in a 'Gold Group', factors that might be considered include: organisational knowledge, specialist discipline, knowledge of the issue and creative ability.

The basic principles behind the 'Gold Group' can work in a wide variety of situations. These can include new product development, dealing with organisational change, resolving production problems and strategic planning. The 'Gold Group' is, however, also a very effective way to deal with a much narrower issue such as absence management.

The first step in bringing a 'Gold Group' together is to identify an individual as the Senior Responsible Officer. This individual is charged with creating the 'Gold Group' and is provided with the freedom to select whoever they believe is most capable of resolving the issue. By nominating someone as the Senior Responsible Officer it is clear to both the individual and the wider organisation that this person has been given the authority to deal with the matter at hand. It also leaves everyone in no doubt that the issue in question has been picked up by the organisation and is viewed seriously enough to empower an individual to form a team dedicated to providing a solution.

The 'Gold Group' is not normally a standing body with full-time staff; rather, it is a collection of individuals who are brought together for the life of a particular issue, to 'PLAN' the investigation and to ultimately identify the solution(s). Individuals who form part of the 'Gold Group' can be allocated specific tasks by the Senior Responsible Officer, but their key role is strategic oversight. It is important, therefore, that the Group does not lose focus by becoming too involved with the rest of the process. For some, involvement in the Gold Group may become a significant distraction from their day job and this needs to be factored into the planning. However, for most people the requirement is simply to attend the 'Gold Group' meeting, provide helpful insights, prompt the wider group and agree actions to be carried out by others.

One additional feature of the 'Gold Group' concept that is interesting to note, is that an invitation to join such a group can have a dramatic impact on an individual. Being specifically selected as someone who can help the organisation to resolve a significant problem or to develop a key initiative can be a major motivator for many. If used sparingly, inclusion in a 'Gold Group' can be seen as bringing a degree of kudos and can send a powerful message to the rest of the organisation.

Having identified the members of the 'Gold Group', the next task of the Senior Responsible Officer is to call the Group together and get them to consider the context of the issue at hand. To do this they will need to review the original 'client' statement, together with the intelligence that has already been collected. The Group will then need to consider the following questions:

What do we know already (or think we know)?

What does this tell us?

What else do we need to know?

Where will we find that information?

How will we get it?

By assessing the intelligence and the original brief in this way, the Group will begin to form an initial understanding of the task at hand. The aim at this stage is to get the 'Gold Group' to use that understanding to develop a series of initial hypotheses as to what the true nature of the problem might be and from this, create a number of potential lines of enquiry.

As you can begin to see, the 'PLAN' phase, so often ignored by organisations, is a vitally important part of the overall framework. Even with something as apparently straightforward as increasing sickness rates, the range of potential scenarios that could be at play are many and varied. For example, it could be that increases in sickness are due to a lack of staff motivation, it could be a problem limited to a given department or region, it could be poor management, it could be poor procedures, or it might be that the record keeping is flawed and the problem does not even exist or is different from the one originally identified. Without planning we would investigate with no clear direction, potentially overlooking valuable evidence, and as a consequence, become distracted by issues that are of no real relevance to finding a lasting solution. Clearly, the 'INITIAL RESPONSE' phase has ensured we have a good understanding of what the 'client' view of the problem is and by 'COLLECTING INTELLIGENCE' we have captured additional information that has helped in forming a more detailed picture. It is, however, the planning undertaken by the 'Gold Group', using their wider knowledge and skills base at a strategic level, that will enable us to interpret that information and develop realistic hypotheses that will ultimately explain what has actually been taking place.

Once the 'Gold Group' has come up with their range of hypotheses the next task is to decide which of these should be pursued and to agree the relevant parameters for gathering the evidence needed to prove or disprove them. The Group will take these decisions after considering all of the intelligence currently available. Examples of possible parameters are: timeframes to use for data sets, the number of people to be interviewed, and the use of external experts. These are all important considerations and help to ensure that an appropriate focus and common understanding is developed before the evidence is sought.

With the hypotheses and parameters in place, the next key task for the Group is to draw up the investigative strategy to be followed. This strategy will be an important document and will be developed by consideration of questions such as:

Do recognised models already exist that can be used to establish the full range of evidence that might be required to arrive at a solution?

How will the integrity of the evidence be maintained? (Remember, once you start looking for evidence people may try to change things in an effort to present a more favourable picture)

How will the evidence be gathered?

Who are the significant witnesses?

Who/what are the main 'suspects'?

What are the risks and consequences associated with the investigation?

The strategy will set out the potential lines of enquiry relevant to each of the hypotheses. For example, a potential hypothesis may be that overall increases in sickness absence can actually be attributed to specific increases in a given category of illness. A line of enquiry for this hypothesis would be to determine whether any one illness category has shown notable increases over and above others. A second line of enquiry related to the same hypothesis may be to establish whether that illness category has gone up uniformly across the whole organisation or is a specific problem in certain regions. The strategy will be developed in line with the agreed parameters and will identify who is responsible for each line of enquiry, what resources they will have available to assist them and what the intended objectives are.

A key point of note is that the investigative strategy must remain under constant review; it should not be seen as set in tablets of stone. The reason for emphasising this point is to ensure that the strategy remains relevant in the light of new unfolding intelligence and evidence, thus we continue to move towards an eventual solution on the basis of all the available facts. Ultimately, investigations by their very nature can be dynamic and fast moving and the 'Gold Group' will need to meet regularly, making both subtle and/or fundamental changes to the original investigative strategy to reflect changes in the direction of the investigation. It is important, therefore, that nobody, especially the Senior Responsible Officer, seeks to hold on to his or her initial hypothesis and defend it against the evidence. To achieve this, it is important that the Group recognises that any such change is not a sign of failure or weakness, rather a demonstration of the value of the investigative technique. Remember; the goal is to find the evidence that leads to a solution, not to reinforce the ego of an individual who believes their 'gut instinct' is always correct.

The final element in 'PLAN' is to draw up a suitable communication strategy. Depending on the circumstances, this may be limited to key stakeholders or widely distributed, both internally and externally, to explain what the organisation is attempting to achieve. The benefit of taking time to address communications at this early stage, is that it enables the organisation to retain control of the message and prevent the rumour mill from going into overdrive, with the ensuing risk this will create for the process. Without a communication strategy the workforce and key stakeholders, both internally and externally, are presented with a vacuum of information. If the issue is of interest, you can guarantee that people will seek to fill that vacuum from other sources. The time and energy that can then be involved in correcting the ensuing misunderstandings will, in all likelihood, far outweigh that required to develop a simple communications strategy from the outset.

I appreciate that this stage in the process can sound rather daunting if you have never tried such a process before.

Perhaps that is why good investigative practice has not readily transferred into the world of work. Without doubt some of the terminology that is used can make the task seem onerous to the uninitiated, but in reality it isn't that complex. If you pick apart what is actually being recommended as part of 'PLAN' and break it down into more simplistic terms then it is difficult to argue that it is anything other than essential. In essence, all we have advocated is a need to pull together a group of people with a range of knowledge and skills, who are best placed to solve the problem, rather than rely on one individual or a single-disciplined team. That group then needs to look at the intelligence the organisation already holds in a structured way, work out what they think is happening and put in place a strategy for getting the evidence they need to either prove or disprove their various theories.

Perhaps perception of the amount of time and planning required is the problem, but it shouldn't be. If one considers that a bad decision in an organisation may lead to significant direct and indirect costs, it doesn't make sense to base decisions on incomplete information and instinct. I appreciate that many managers pride themselves on their 'gut instinct' and seek to use their experience as a shield, but they miss the point. 'Gut instinct' is still required in this process, it is a vital part of developing hypotheses; however, 'gut instinct' should be checked against the facts and, if it proves misguided, the manager needs to accept that fact and use their experience to identify other more plausible explanations that are supported by the evidence.

The mistake made by many organisations is that they never see an issue such as sickness absence as deserving of this level of attention. Whilst most recognise that sickness has a direct impact on the 'bottom line', they simply turn to the HR Director or the manager of the 'problem' area and demand that things get better. In the short-term this might work, but it is an approach that falls well short if you are aiming to maximise your chance of developing a sustainable solution. If we go back and look at the direct and indirect cost of absence that we identified earlier, then the need for a properly planned intervention as advocated by this book could not be logically argued against.

'Real World Approach' - Plan

'Well Marcus, that was an interesting meeting' said the Chief Executive. 'I thought Joe was about to explode at one point, but you needn't worry about him, he's a sweetie really, just gets all defensive if anyone says anything remotely critical about his beloved Operations function. So what do you need to complete this little investigation of yours?'

'I need a working group to review the background intelligence with me and then prepare a proper investigative plan.'

Helen looked a little perplexed. 'I'm not sure I really get it Marcus, what's the difference between intelligence and investigation?'

Marcus set about explaining. 'Background intelligence gives you an indication of the best places to start looking if you want to solve a problem. Even with something as narrow as sickness absence, the full list of potential reasons why it might be increasing are huge and if you start following every possible lead you will get totally lost. What you do is gather some intelligence by looking at data, talking to people, checking what is happening on the ground and analysing what the position is in the wider world. From this we develop a limited number of hypotheses of the best places to look for our solution and these form the basis for the investigation. The investigation itself then provides the evidence to either prove or disprove the various hypotheses.'

'Well that sounds a bit more professional than what we normally do around here, but how long will it take?'

'That's the surprising thing, it actually takes no longer than normal, in fact it will stop us running off and wasting time and money chasing solutions that aren't related to the real problem. The trick is to keep an open mind and to follow the evidence. As soon as the evidence proves your hypothesis is wrong you either amend it or drop it and develop a new hypothesis based on where the evidence has led you'

'Okay, I'm sold' replied Helen. 'I'll back you, but I need results on this. Who do you want to work with you?'

'It's got to be people who can make a real difference to the outcome. Some will need to get involved because of their role in the organisation, but it's more about getting a group together who have real organisational credibility. If you want results I need a good mix of people; some will require detailed organisational knowledge, but it's also important that I also get people with strategic insight and the ability to be creative and free-thinking, regardless of their existing role or

69

experience.

'So you want the cream of the organisation. Well I can quite understand why, but I can't afford to release them, they've got day jobs to do. You are just going to have to get on with it using your own staff and whoever I can get released by the Divisions.

'I appreciate the problem' said Marcus 'but I don't need them released from their day job, their role isn't full-time. It will just be a brief meeting once a week to keep an eye on progress and help to develop the thinking on this issue; my staff will do the running around and actually conduct the investigation. It's their brains and insight I'm looking to capitalise on, think of them as the organisation's 'golden boys', all brought together in one group to solve the organisation's biggest problem.'

'A bit sexist, but I like it. My golden group; I tell you what, let's call it the "Gold Group" that will get everyone talking, much better than asking people to be part of the sickness reduction working party.'

Marcus knew a good thing when he saw it. 'Okay I'll get started straight away.'

Later that same day Marcus sat down with Bob Ainsworth and together they began to identify the individuals that they felt were capable of dispassionately reviewing the collected intelligence and also had the ability and/or the clout to help develop the investigation and keep it on track. Looking at the finished list, it had people from different levels, different departments and different skill sets. Amongst them were some of the brightest new talent as well as a smattering of "heavyweight" movers and shakers.

The invites went out, making it clear that people were being invited by the Chief Executive to be part of a "Gold Group" to deal with a major issue that the organisation was aiming to address. It had the desired effect; the term "Gold Group" was causing something of a stir, people looked at the list of those being brought together and one or two began to enviously question why they are not part of it. It was clear to everyone that this was a Group that would get things done.

At the first meeting, Marcus set out the problem that they had been brought together to solve. Sickness has been on the increase and the Chief Executive wanted the trend reversed. Some new initiatives had already been put in place to deal with stress and muscular skeletal absence, but in gathering together all of the background information, it had become clear that under-recording of sickness was a problem in

Operations and possibly across the whole organisation and this needed to be addressed during the investigation.

The group began to look through the intelligence that had been gathered and almost immediately Amy, a trainee from Research and Development, put Marcus on the spot. 'How extensive is this problem of under-recording, I can't find mention of it here in the paperwork?'

'It looks as though it might be very wide-spread' was the answer. 'I've spoken to a few individuals who have highlighted it as an issue.'

'Yes, but how widespread and how much impact is it having on the organisations overall sickness figure. Surely we can't just follow a bit of gossip and base our decisions on that.'

'You are right Amy' replied Marcus 'we can't make decisions for the future based on information that we haven't tested, but we can use organisational stories such as these to help shape the investigation. That's the beauty of intelligence, it enables us to look at the issue in the widest possible context and then pick out those factors that we should focus on when we go out to gather evidence. I believe from what I've heard that we've got a problem with under-reporting, but I accept that at the moment I don't have the evidence to prove that it's the cause of our current sickness absence issues.'

The Group continued through the rest of the intelligence pack that they'd been given and then began to identify the most likely hypotheses for the increase in sickness. 'Remember,' said Marcus, 'you are all here because you have something to offer, we need everyone to contribute to this debate. It's important that you set out your pet ideas, your gut reaction to what you've seen, then we'll work through them all and come up with a number of hypotheses that we can test.'

Amy jumped in again. 'What if we don't pick the right hypothesis? Surely we will just miss the solution? Why don't we follow all of the leads we have, that way we can't be wrong?'

'In reality, we don't have the resource in terms of staffing or time to follow every lead to its conclusion, the cost would be huge. We won't miss the solution; if the evidence shows a hypothesis is wrong we will adjust it or drop it in favour of another until we have the answer. Don't forget we will be working to very specific lines of enquiry to ensure the investigations are focused. That way we won't get led up a garden path by simply chasing the latest bit of information. If you think about it, that's what normally happens and is why lasting solutions are few and far between when you are looking at complex issues such as this. This time we will be following a proper planning process.'

'All seems a bit like a police investigation to me,' said Fred Churchill from Marketing. 'You looking to catch some people?'

'It's exactly like a police investigation, but I'm not looking to catch people, just solve the issue. If you think about it, all we are doing is putting a structured problem-solving process in place that makes sure we get to the right outcome. How many times have you faced something like this and just run with your gut reaction or shaped the evidence to fit what you already believe? What we are doing today is assessing the intelligence, deciding from that the most likely cause of the problem and then going out to investigate whether our judgment is right. If it isn't, we just come back here and start the planning process again.'

'I like it' said Fred. It's got a neatness and logic to it you can see how it all fits in. Let's get started and agree these hypo-thingamajigs then we can get the investigations started.'

An hour later the Group had come up with three hypotheses that were thought to be the likely cause of sickness absence increasing. These were:

74

1. There has been widespread under-reporting of sickness absence and this was preventing the organisation from fundamentally reducing its absence levels.

2. The increase in sickness levels over the past 12 months was directly related to an increase in the amount of stress related absence and would be reduced by specific health initiatives and closer management of those specific cases.

3. Sickness levels were generally up across the organisation and there was no specific cause.

The Group then agreed the overall parameters for the investigation. They agreed to limit the review to the last 12 months, as this was the timeframe highlighted by the Chief Executive. It was also felt that all regions and departments should be involved in the review, but at this stage it shouldn't extend to Anywhere Inc.'s sister company.

Specific lines of enquiry were then established. For the first hypothesis these were:

1. To establish how much under-reporting of absence exists.

2. To determine whether under-reporting was an organisation wide problem or limited to certain functions.

3. To identify precisely how under-reporting was preventing better management of sickness absence.

A specific lead was allocated for each line of enquiry and they were provided with actions that were to be completed and reported back to the "Gold Group". For the first line of enquiry, 'how much under-reporting of absence exists', the objectives were as follows:

1. Gather sickness data records for the past 12 months.

2. Compare the sickness data against time sheets/shift records/overtime records.

3. Estimate the level of under-reporting.

It was agreed that there was a need to keep progress under regular review and the Group agreed to meet on a weekly basis so they could adjust, or if necessary drop, any hypothesis that wasn't consistent with the facts. They could also adjust the lines of enquiry and actions as new evidence came to light, to make sure that the investigation remained relevant and on-track.

Marcus was happy with the progress that had been made. He was particularly pleased that his own pet theory had made it through to the final three hypotheses to be reviewed. There had been some resistance around the room, which Marcus put down to a fear of Joe Shiner and the power of the Operations

Department, but in the end there was a consensus view that this should be followed up.

'Listen,' said Fred, 'I know some of us have already got quite strong views regarding the cause of the problem, but we must be prepared to follow the evidence and change our position if necessary. Otherwise we are wasting our time, isn't that right Marcus? What matters is we get to the correct solution, not whose gut instinct was right or wrong.'

The Group agreed and decided that it would be beneficial if the discussions stayed in the room, as that would help people to adjust their position more easily. Whilst agreeing with the sentiment, Marcus wanted to make sure that an information vacuum wasn't created. Everyone accepted that a communications strategy would be a sensible way forward and this was tasked out as an action from the meeting. To ensure early rumour control was in place, it was agreed that part one of the strategy would be a simple news item placed on the intranet stating that a Gold Group had been formed by the Chief Executive to review sickness absence and to determine if there was scope to improve processes, thereby increasing productivity and reducing costs.

Summary – Plan

1. Appoint a Senior Responsible Officer

2. Form a 'Gold Group'.

3. Review the intelligence:

    a. What do we know already (or think we know)?

    b. What does this tell us?

    c. What else do we need to know?

    d. Where will we find the evidence?

    e. How do we get it?

4. Develop hypotheses and potential lines of enquiry.

5. Set parameters for the investigation.

6. Set the investigative strategy.

7. Set the communications strategy.

CHAPTER 6

Gather Evidence

Phase 4: Gather Evidence

It was highlighted earlier in the book that many organisations do not get past 'INITIAL RESPONSE' , they grab at quick wins and limit their focus to those matters perceived as critical and in need of immediate attention. This often results in those self same organisations missing the underlying issues and failing to deliver sustained improvement. Where an organisation does go further, the temptation is often to immediately jump to 'GATHER EVIDENCE', in the false hope that this will quickly lead to a meaningful solution. What this fails to recognise is that a good investigation is invariably based on sound intelligence and effective planning. If you have jumped straight from 'INITIAL RESPONSE' to this section, viewing it as the most important, I would strongly encourage you to go back and follow the earlier phases of 'COLLECT INTELLIGENCE' and 'PLAN'. Without these, you risk overlooking valuable evidence and could find the investigation becomes derailed, either deliberately or accidentally, as a result of distractions and following issues that are of no real relevance.

Assuming that you have heeded the advice and followed all of the phases of the process in sequence, you will already be aware that the investigative strategy, created during 'PLAN', is an important document and will dictate how we conduct the investigation and 'GATHER EVIDENCE'. Remember, that we set that strategy to reflect the hypotheses developed by the 'Gold Group' and use it to indicate how the various lines of enquiry are to be pursued.

In the 'real world' example we are following in this book, one of the hypotheses put forward by the 'Gold Group' was that sickness absence had been under-reported and this was preventing the organisation from truly understanding the issue and putting in place the mechanisms to fundamentally reduce its absence levels. The lines of enquiry resulting from that hypothesis were:

1. To establish how much under-reporting was occurring;

2. To determine whether under-reporting was happening uniformly across the organisation;

3. To establish what, if anything, was driving that under-reporting.

Set out at 'Figure 1' is an example of how an investigative strategy document might be set out to cover these points. It includes details of who has been allocated the line of enquiry, what resources they have been provided with and what specific objectives are to be delivered.

It is important to remember that each investigative strategy will be unique. Who we need to interview and what data we

Hypothesis	There has been widespread under-reporting of sickness absence and this was preventing the organisation from fundamentally reducing its absence levels.
Line of Enquiry 1	Establish how much under-reporting occurs
Allocated	Alice Brown
Resources	Clive Smith
Objectives	By 1 July 2013: Gather sickness data records for the past 12 months Compare sickness data against time sheets/shift records/overtime records; Estimate level of under-reporting.
Line of Enquiry 2	Is under-reporting uniform across the organisation?
Allocated	Peter Davis
Resources	Helen Richards
Objectives	By 1 July 2013: Interview a representative cross-section of managers about their knowledge of under-reporting; Interview a representative cross-section of staff about their knowledge of under-reporting; Hold focus group meetings within each major division to discuss under-reporting; Estimate distribution of under-reporting across the organisation.

Figure 1

need to gather will depend on the hypothesis we are dealing with and the lines of enquiry being followed. It is also important to remember that evidence can come from observation and real life examples just as easily as it comes from interviews and focus groups. The overflowing in-box, the constantly ringing phone and the increase in customer complaints can all potentially provide useful sources of evidence. Recognise, however, that there may be some who will not like the findings and will seek to challenge the evidence; consequently, proper record keeping is an essential element of the process. If a challenge is made, you need to be clear about how you have come to a given viewpoint and be in a position to identify the specific evidence that led to that outcome. By having clear records of the evidence to hand, it is possible to work out whether it is right to defend a given point or whether to adjust your position; in doing so the evidential records will help you understand the impact on the wider investigation.

Remember, if you need to interview individuals as part of an investigation, some may be worried about providing evidence and feel uncomfortable about talking to you unless they are given certain assurances about anonymity. Ultimately, it is for the 'client' to determine how they wish to approach this issue as there are likely to be a variety of factors to take into account depending on the organisation and issue at hand. Before beginning any interview it is, therefore, beneficial to clarify this matter for all concerned to avoid any potential impact on confidence in the investigation and its eventual outcome.

Once the evidence has been gathered, you need to take steps to ensure that it can be validated or at least make an informed judgment regarding its reliability, just as we did for the intelligence we gathered earlier in the process. For example, if an individual is providing information that just does not correlate to anything else, then you have to consider its accuracy. It does not automatically mean it is incorrect, but you do need to follow the trail of evidence and attempt to triangulate the information in an effort to validate its reliability. Conversely, you may wish to apply additional weight to a piece of evidence where you fundamentally trust the source even though there is little to verify its accuracy. Whilst you do not need to ignore such uncorroborated information, it is best to recognise that the value of such evidence is often weakened, particularly when subject to later challenge; therefore, there is a need to reflect on the advisability of its inclusion.

As highlighted in 'PLAN', it is necessary to keep the investigative strategy under constant review as the investigation progresses. This is to ensure that the strategy remains relevant in the light of new evidence as it unfolds. Once the investigation starts, the 'Gold Group' will be meeting regularly to review the evidence as it is collected and consider the progress being made. As they perform this role, they will frequently find it necessary to return to the original investigative strategy and make either subtle or fundamental changes to reflect alterations in the direction of the investigation. Clearly, this further reinforces the need to keep proper records of evidence as you go through the 'GATHER EVIDENCE' phase. This will help avoid confusion and speed up the process if it becomes necessary to return to an earlier hypothesis or line of enquiry that had previously been discarded.

What is important as you 'GATHER EVIDENCE' is to keep the focus on the agreed strategy and not get distracted. It is for the 'Gold Group' to consider all of the evidence and decide if a change of direction is necessary. If those carrying out the investigation are allowed to simply deviate from the plan whenever they see fit, it is unlikely that you will come to a meaningful conclusion that is supported by fact. That is not to say that the investigator remains blinkered, rather that they should follow their line of enquiry as planned and simply report back any supplementary information that they have come across and allow the Group to consider what weight to give it, rather than get side-tracked and fail to deliver on the objectives that have been set.

'Real World Approach' – Gather Evidence

With the investigative strategy agreed, Marcus returned to his office and called in the members of his staff who would be acting as leads for each line of enquiry. Having explained the task at hand and set out the investigative strategy to be followed, Marcus described the difficulties that can be created when people don't understand the ground rules that apply when they provide evidence.

'Many people are happy to play things straight and just say what they think, while others, out of a sense of loyalty or fear, try to hide evidence or present it in a more favourable light. To complicate matters still further there are also those who may be too frightened to say anything or simply try to mislead the investigation for their own ends.'

To help address some of these issues, Marcus handed out a letter signed by the Chief Executive, which was to be given to everyone who was spoken to. The document confirmed the anonymity of those providing evidence, explained the organisation's aims and requested that individuals helped as best they could. Despite this, Marcus made it clear to his staff that, where possible, they were to take steps to validate the reliability of the evidence by crosschecking against other sources, including their own observations.

By the end of the first week, Marcus was ready to call the Gold Group back together to review the evidence obtained to-date. Whilst it was still early days in the investigation, the data on stress related absence had already been obtained and demonstrated that although it was the most common cause of long-term absence, its levels hadn't actually increased in the last 12 months.

The Group considered the hypothesis relating to this point:

The increase in sickness levels in the past 12 months is directly related to an increase in the amount of stress related absence and could be reduced by specific health initiatives and closer management of those specific cases.

Clearly, the evidence didn't support this hypothesis. Some in the group called for the investigation to be widened by looking at trends over a longer period of time, as they were sure this was a major factor and shared stories of cases known to them that had caused significant difficulties.

Marcus brought them all back to the agreed parameters of the investigation. 'When we completed the planning process we agreed a number of limitations to the investigation, one of which was to review the data over the last 12 months as this was the timeframe set by the Chief Executive. I agree that a longer-term review of stress may be beneficial, but that must be a separate exercise and not part of this investigation, otherwise we will confuse the issue. We now know that it isn't the cause of the recent increases in sickness absence so let's stick with what we said last week and follow the evidence.'

The Group agreed to halt further investigation linked to that particular hypothesis and to free up the resource that had been allocated to its associated actions. No new hypotheses came forward from the evidence, so after only half an hour the members of the Group were heading back to their day jobs agreeing to meet again in a week's time to look at any further developments relating to the remaining hypotheses.

By week two, a considerable amount of information was beginning to flow in for the Gold Group to consider. The review of sickness data against time sheets, overtime records and shift records was not showing a problem with under-recording of sickness. This was backed up by the information from the interviews and the focus group with managers and staff, which identified they was no knowledge of any problem. There was one exception, however, a member of staff from a team in the Operations Division had anonymously complained of excessive workload, as a result of covering for other staff. A check of records for that team had made interesting reading, it showed high levels of overtime compared to other sections and the timesheets for some staff were missing.

Marcus was not happy. 'This just has to be wrong. I spoke to some managers and a trade union official when this sickness issue first came up and they clearly said there was widespread under-reporting.'

'That isn't what the evidence shows' said Amy. 'We need to lose this hypothesis.'

'Not yet,' said Marcus, 'I want to push this point further. I've still got a gut feeling about this, just give it another week and set some additional objectives for that particular line of enquiry, including specifically interviewing the trade union rep and those managers I spoke to previously.'

With some reluctance the Group agreed and came back to the issue one week later.

'Sorry boss,' said Bob, the HR Business Partner, as he began his update to the group. 'I know you were hoping that this was the answer, but I've interviewed those people you asked me to and apart from the union rep they deny all knowledge of saying under-reporting is a widespread problem. As for the union rep, she reaffirmed that it is a problem, but the only evidence she could give related to that disciplinary case in Operations that you were dealing with and the person that came forward with the anonymous complaint came from that same team. It looks like it's an isolated issue and isn't having an impact of any note on the figures.'

Marcus was stuck; his pet theory looked to be blown out of the water and he would need to downgrade the risk he had originally identified. Joe Shiner was going to be unbearable at the next Board Meeting, it was so tempting to keep pushing the issue despite the evidence, but Marcus knew that wasn't right and would deflect them from the true solution. 'Okay, lets take a look at the rest of the evidence and see where it takes us. It looks like we only have one hypothesis left and that's the rather unexciting position that sickness is just generally higher across the board'

'I'm afraid,' said Bob, 'that we don't even have that. Sickness levels differ quite markedly across the organisation if you look at job type. There's one more thing; it seems clear from the interviews I've been holding that our records aren't accurate.'

Marcus look confused and just a little bit flustered. 'You've just told the Group the records are accurate, that we didn't have any under-recording apart from one small team.'

'That's correct but what our interviews have uncovered, and it's backed up by the data, some of the bigger departments like Operations have been misclassifying lots of records. You remember that the Chief Executive was focused on a problem with back injuries at one of the factories? Well she appears to have created a minor miracle. Since that became an issue, Operations have not recorded a single day of absence under the code for muscular skeletal injuries.'

Suddenly Marcus perked up. 'Okay I think we might be getting somewhere. Lets take a look at our two remaining hypotheses and see how they might need adjusting and then lets get out there and get the remaining evidence that will prove which, if any, of these theories are correct.'

The Group sat down to review the three hypotheses that they had started with:

There has been widespread under-reporting of sickness absence and this was preventing the organisation from fundamentally reducing its absence levels.

The increase in sickness levels in the last 12 months was directly related to an increase in the amount of stress related absence and would be reduced by specific health initiatives and closer management of those specific cases.

Sickness levels were generally up across the organisation and there was no specific cause.

Hypothesis number 2 had already been discounted. The remaining two were now amended to reflect the evidence that had now been uncovered and now read:

There has been a widespread miscoding of sickness absence and this has prevented the organisation from fundamentally reducing its absence levels;

Sickness rates are up as a result of poor attendance rates in some but not all job types.

The Group updated the investigative strategy to reflect the revised hypotheses and agreed to meet again in one week's time, when they hoped to have sufficient evidence to identify a solution.

'I do like this process,' said Fred, 'it's just like those detective programmes on the T.V. We started with three potential reasons for our problem, but it turns out that none of them where right. Now we've refined them as a result of the evidence we've been given and are looking for a different solution. It's a nice change to be doing this properly, we'd probably have locked the wrong person up by now if we'd done our usual running around.'

There was an air of expectancy around the room when the Group got back together the following week. When they were originally formed, some had queried why they had to be involved and one or two had serious reservations about being part of something that had such a daft tag as 'Gold Group'. These views had, however, dissipated very quickly; it was clear to them that they had been hand-picked to solve a key problem for the organisation and that they were there to be heard and to shape the outcome, not merely to make up the numbers in a 'talking shop'.

The leads for the various lines of enquiry presented their evidence and the Group collated this against the previous evidence they had received and began to review the remaining hypotheses.

'It looks like we have our answer' said Penny Allison the Exchequer Manager. 'The data is clearly showing that in the last twelve months there have been big increases in sickness in four quite distinct job groups and we have also had significant miscoding of sickness in Operations'.

Amy was less convinced. 'Okay, I accept we have two issues at play here that need to be addressed, but are we sure they are the main cause of the increase we have seen recently.'

'I agree with you Amy,' said Marcus, 'look at the evidence. There is no increase in sickness in Operations over the last 12 months; in fact their sickness has gone down. Their lack of accurate records isn't acceptable, but it's not part of the solution to this particular problem; I will deal with that separately. The issue in terms of increased sickness is down to those four specific job groups and we've missed them before because the sickness data is focused on divisions and regions.'

Fred was ready to go. 'So that's it then we're done, you just report that back to the Chief and we all get a pat on the back for solving this issue, isn't that how it works?'

'Well, we do seem to have a clear outcome. Whilst there might be other factors at play, I think we are all confident that the evidence is here to prove beyond reasonable doubt what the problem is. What we don't have yet though is a solution, this is just the identification of the cause.'

Summary – Gather Evidence

1. Follow the investigative strategy.

2. Set out the ground rules in advance for those providing evidence.

3. Use observation and 'real life' as well as interviews and data for your evidence sources.

4. Take steps to validate the reliability of the evidence obtained.

5. Test the hypotheses as you go.

6. If dictated by the evidence, return to the planning phase.

7. Don't get distracted.... follow the plan - adjust it if necessary, but follow the evidence.

CHAPTER 7

Develop Solution

Phase 5: Develop Solution

A common mistake made in many investigations is to move too early to a solution. Presented with evidence that points in the general direction of a given answer, there is always a temptation to jump to a particular conclusion in an effort to shorten the process. No matter how small that leap is, making such a move is always a mistake. You should only progress to developing a solution when the answer to the issue is proven 'beyond reasonable doubt'.

The problem with making the call too early is that valuable evidence might be missed. You are, therefore, operating in the absence of all the available facts. If your chosen solution is ultimately shown to be flawed and there is clear and readily available evidence that confirms an alternative answer, it can be difficult and in some cases impossible, to go back and continue with the previous investigation. It is almost inevitable that you will have undermined your position and this could lead to your judgment being called into question. Even if the evidence isn't something that would have resulted in a different answer, it may be such that it fundamentally alters the nature of the required solution. Again, this is a difficult point to recover from if you have begun investing time, money and personal credibility in an alternative outcome. It is, therefore, vital to take your time when investigating and properly assess all of the relevant intelligence and evidence against the hypotheses to ensure the answer when decided upon is the correct one.

Once an appropriate answer does present itself, it is advisable to re-validate the evidence that you will be relying upon. Remember there will be a need to ensure that the evidence can stand up to challenge and scrutiny from others. This doesn't need to be a long winded or complex process, just go back and look at the key evidence, where possible triangulate it by looking for suitable corroboration from other sources, then consider the reliability of both the source and the information provided and make a considered assessment.

When you are happy with the evidence, consider if any other hypothesis could possibly provide the same answer. For example, lets assume your hypothesis is that absence has increased as a result of back pain due to working practices in the area concerned and the evidence confirms this. That same evidence may also support an alternative hypothesis, namely that the extent of absence related to back pain is the result of poor absence management processes for that particular illness. If there is doubt or uncertainty regarding which hypothesis is correct don't be frightened to go back to 'PLAN' and revise the investigative strategy in order to gather the evidence to prove which answer is correct.

Ultimately, it is far better to take slightly longer and rule out other possible answers, than to waste time attempting to defend an outcome that has been announced too early and then meets with a number of detractors. All too often in organisations, the desire to chase the quick win and move on to the next issue creates the potential for failure and disharmony. In reality, there are very few solutions to organisational problems that are completely without opposition, whether it be individual self-interest, internal power politics or just ideological differences; somebody, somewhere, will question the answer you come up with if the opportunity presents itself. Don't be surprised if late in the day others attempt to promote alternative answers. If you have done your job properly this shouldn't be a problem, you will have the hard evidence to prove 'beyond reasonable doubt' that the answer you are advocating is the correct one.

It is often helpful, in this phase of the process, to think of yourself as a prosecuting lawyer when deciding whether you have enough evidence to support a given solution as the right one. Imagine that the defence is testing your evidence and consider whether it is strong enough to result in a conviction.

Remember, you may well have identified the correct guilty party, but if the evidence doesn't stand up to scrutiny the case will be lost and it will be the weakest piece of evidence that will be the focus of the challenge, not the strongest. Your defence will be the logic of your argument and the weight of the evidence that stands behind it.

Assuming that you have an answer that you are happy with and the evidence to justify that conclusion, it is now time to develop the solution. In many ways this can be the most satisfying part of the whole process. With a clear understanding of what is causing the absence problem, it is now possible to put all of that hard work to good effect by finding a solution that is sustainable into the future.

Your search for a solution should normally involve an assessment of existing best practice. There is no point re-inventing the wheel when you can 'borrow with pride' from someone who has already spent the time building a well thought out and effective solution. If you have taken the advice set out at Phase 2 'COLLECT INTELLIGENCE', there will already be an environmental scan in place and this is a good place to start looking for possible sources of best practice.

If a ready solution isn't available then it's time to get creative. Work through the development of your solution from first principles. You know the answer to the issue and, therefore, the required outcome. It may be that an existing product can provide a partial solution and just needs minor amendment to produce a more appropriate fit but, if not, don't be frightened to think 'outside the box' and develop something that is bespoke to the issue you face. Remember, you have the hard evidence to back up the assessment of what the answer to the problem is, so you can afford to really push the boundaries in terms of a solution when you are on such firm ground.

If there are lots of potential solutions that appear to provide the necessary solution, then it is probably advisable to develop an options appraisal and look at the costs and anticipated benefits associated with each to determine which solution to take forward and 'IMPLEMENT'. Where possible, it is always advisable to test your chosen solution to ensure it produces the desired effect. Whilst it can sometimes take time for a solution to have its intended impact, a limited pilot project can help to iron out future implementation difficulties and avoid any unintended consequences.

'Real World Approach' – Develop Solution

'This is where you can really help me given I'm new to the organisation', Marcus began. 'We now have the evidence to prove what the cause of the increase in sickness is attributable to, so it's time to develop an appropriate solution. I've got ideas and techniques that I've used before in other organisations and Bob found some new techniques being used elsewhere when he did the environmental scan. However, I don't want to create any unintended consequences due to a lack of organisational understanding. I need to know culturally whether the proposed solutions fit here and what barriers I might need to overcome to put them in place. If everyone is happy I will work up a detailed set of options and present them at our next meeting.'

'Whilst you do that, can we get your staff to double check the accuracy and reliability of the evidence that we are relying upon' said Amy. 'I know that it's already been looked at as they collected it, but it would be good to just reassure ourselves that nothing has been missed.'

'Absolutely, I'll get Bob to go over everything again just in case.'

Fred was impressed. 'You do realise we are in danger of actually doing this properly don't you? When the Chief Executive originally called you in and asked you for an improvement plan to reverse the increase in sickness rates, you jumped in with a couple of quick solutions, normally that's where we stop.'

'Yes, but I knew it would need more than that; I didn't just stop there. I got hold of as much background intelligence as possible, so I could find out what was really going on' replied Marcus.

'And that was the right thing to do; that gave us the information we needed to work out what the problem might be and meant we could plan a proper investigation. If we had just followed our original instincts, we would never have arrived at this point, we would be building a solution for a different problem.'

'You're right,' agreed Bob, 'and what's most striking is that it hasn't actually taken much more effort than I would normally put in to deal with something like this. When you think about how we stopped some of our lines of enquiry very early on and revised our hypotheses as new evidence came to light, we've probably saved valuable time. Instead of wasting time running after pet theories, we've followed a structured approach and based the outcome on hard evidence. Now we can design a solution that we can be confident will address the problem.'

'But what would have happened if it hadn't worked, if there was no answer?' queried Amy.

'We would have just gone back and started the planning process all over again and if necessary gone out to gather more background intelligence to support a completely different set of theories' said Marcus. He was really enthused; he knew he had a group of converts for this structured approach to looking at organisational problems. 'We've all been in situations where you face a problem, you know you should investigate it, but you find a quick win or latch on to some data that proves your own theory and just hope it's the right thing to do, invariably it rarely is. You can use this model for almost anything, developing a new product, finding out why an important customer has cut their order, whatever the problem the process of getting to a meaningful solution is the same'.

'So how did you come across this process then?' asked the Exchequer Manager.

'My brother is a detective. He works on all sorts of different cases, some of them are so complex and involved that I would often listen in amazement when he told me how they had solved the case. I began to ask how they even knew where to start and he explained the structured process they would follow. It then struck me that we regularly faced difficult cases in organisations and that whilst the context was different, the approach we needed to follow was basically the same. It just seemed to make sense to me, the world of work is so competitive that there isn't room for mistakes. We need to make sure that our solutions are built on sound evidence, so what could be better than to follow a process that a professional investigator would use?'

'Well it makes perfect sense to me,' said Penny, 'I'm just glad I got selected for this group. I can't wait to try this approach again. It feels like I've really learnt a new skill that I can make use of again and again.'

The following week the Group got together for the last time. Marcus presented them with options for dealing with the four staffing groups that were causing a problem and apart from a few minor tweaks in terms of how best to present the findings, they all agreed it was a sensible approach that everyone should be able to buy into.

'What happens next?' said Amy.

'Well I present this to the Chief Executive and make sure I've got her buy-in and then I'll take it to the wider Board. After that, assuming they go with it, I'll set up the implementation and take a look at how we prevent the problem from recurring in future.' Marcus started to go into full speech mode 'I'd just like to thank you all for everything that you've done, it's been a real team effort.'

'Don't, I'll start to well up' laughed Fred. 'Just make sure to remember us when they start dishing out the performance payments!'

Marcus headed off to meet the Chief Executive and to go through the outcomes from the investigation and the details of the solution to the problem.

When he had finished presenting the information, the Chief Executive smiled. 'I'm impressed. It's taken slightly longer than normal, but I can see that's because you've looked at the problem thoroughly and based the solution on hard evidence. Well done Marcus, I'm glad my idea for the "Gold Group" came together so well.'

Later that week, Marcus presented the report to the rest of the Board. If Joe Shiner didn't agree with the way forward, he didn't show it. That might have been because the Chief Executive was clearly happy with the solution, or it might be that he didn't was to raise his head above the parapet after Bob Ainsworth had told him about the mis-recording of sickness in Operations. Either way Marcus was glad that everyone supported his proposals.

The Finance Director was particularly glowing. 'I did some work on the figures last night, just to work out some rough estimates in terms of cost-benefit analysis. I'd originally thought we would need to make some significant reductions in sickness if we were to fund that Gold Group, but that just wasn't the case. You had a total of 8 people on the group, you met for approximately 1 hour each week for 6 weeks, so that's not even a day's pay. By my reckoning we have 4,000 staff and if we could save a day on our sickness average figures that is 4,000 days pay or the cost of about 20 full-time staff for a year. I reckon that's a bargain, even allowing for the staff time used in carrying out the investigations.

'We would have paid that out anyway,' replied Marcus. 'The problem wasn't going to go away it needed investigating. By structuring the process properly we avoided wasting time in developing solutions for a problem that didn't really exist'.

'I think you've really got something here,' said the Chief Executive. 'Next time we have a problem I'm going to set up one of those "Gold Groups" and follow this process. Don't you agree Marcus has developed a really useful operational tool Joe?'

'Yeah, yeah, bloke's a regular genius.'

Marcus ignored the gibe and summed up. 'Our next step is to make sure we implement the solution properly, then we'll review how things have gone over the next few quarters to see if the solution has worked. It's likely to take a little time for the initiatives to start impacting on the figures, but provided everything works as expected we should see a sustained improvement. The other thing I'm going to do is to take a look at why the issue arose in the first place so we can take steps to prevent an issue like this from ever happening again.'

Summary – Develop Solution

1. Only move to DEVELOP SOLUTION when the answer to the issue is proven 'beyond reasonable doubt'.

2. Double-check the accuracy and reliability of the evidence.

3. Consider if any other hypothesis could provide the same answer.

4. Search for examples of proven 'best practice' and be prepared to 'borrow with pride'.

5. If a ready solution isn't available, be creative and develop your own.

6. Develop option appraisals if relevant.

7. Test your chosen solution to ensure it produces the desired effect.

8. If you cannot prove the issue 'beyond reasonable doubt' return to PLAN.

CHAPTER 8

Implement

Phase 6: Implement

Once you have identified a solution, your next step is to deal with the implementation process. The reason why 'IMPLEMENT' is a phase in it's own right and not part of 'DEVELOP SOLUTION' is because of the fundamental importance of good implementation to a successful outcome. Ultimately, you may have the correct solution, but if the implementation is flawed you are unlikely to achieve the intended outcome. Even where there is overwhelming evidence that you have chosen the correct path, a failure to consider implementation issues in a meaningful way can prove fatal.

If you have found your solution and the evidence to back it up, the first thing you need to do, as part of the implementation, is to communicate that fact; don't be shy!! Remember, your enemy at this point is silence. If you don't say anything, don't be surprised when others with a vested interest make up their own stories, to fill the void that has been allowed to develop. Left to their own devices, it is amazing how wildly inaccurate such messages can become. Don't forget, the longer the silence the more difficult recovery can become. Be proactive; tell people what you've found and what you're going to do about it.

In preparing your message you need to think about your target audience and how the message will be received if you are to maximise understanding and avoid any potential for resistance. That means, amongst other things, deciding on the tone of the message, the media to be used and the frequency of that communication. It is a good idea to set up a basic communications strategy to help with this process and there are plenty of examples that can be found so pick one that fits the culture of your organisation. When well thought out, a communications strategy is rarely a waste of time and more often than not it provides the foundations on which you can 'IMPLEMENT' the solution.

Unfortunately, in some situations, the message you have to convey and the solution you propose will not be welcome. If you are faced with such a dilemma, then it is important that you identify the extent of the likely problem, as this will enable you to plan how best to overcome, or at least minimise the issue. In some extreme circumstances, it may be necessary to consider bypassing resistance in order to gain a level of momentum behind your chosen solution and allow you to move forward, but wherever possible be as open and honest as possible. A rationale adult-to-adult conversation is invariably the best way forward.

The next element of the 'IMPLEMENT' phase is to develop the implementation plan. This can range from a fully blown project plan, to the simple identification of a number of tasks to be undertaken. In all but the most straightforward of solutions, however, there will be a need for some form of planning, as there will be actions that need to take place over an extended period of time. For example, the chosen solution may require culture change, investment in new technology or development of a training programme, none of which will occur immediately or without investment. Depending on the size of the solution to be implemented, it may be necessary to set up a dedicated project team who are charged with delivery and monitoring progress to ensure the entire solution is completed according to plan.

There is a lot of theory and good practice already in existence in relation to effective project management, so I will not go over it here. However, whatever the extent of the project to be undertaken, one thing you will almost inevitably want to do is to identify quick wins and those actions that can be implemented at an early stage. It can be an important sign to the organisation, its staff, managers and other interested parties that things are changing. If chosen correctly, these early signs can be a powerful demonstration of progress and create a steamroller effect that helps with the remainder of the implementation.

Once the project plan has been implemented, you need to take steps to embed the 'new normality' to avoid the potential for slipping back into bad habits. Embedding this new normality can take many forms and involve varying degrees of subtlety. For example, the Chief Executive in praising the action of an early adopter at a meeting can send out a gentle message to others present that this is the behaviour they wish to see followed. Issuing higher performance payments and providing promotions to those most closely associated as advocates of the new normality offers an even more direct form of reinforcement. What is important is to ensure consistency of message and to make use of all relevant opportunities to reinforce that message. Don't forget, posters on the back of toilet doors and computer screen-savers, are often read by more people than the company magazine!!

'Real World Approach' – Implement

Marcus left the Boardroom a happy man. He returned to the office to find Bob Ainsworth waiting for him.

'How was that?' asked Bob

'Absolutely marvellous, no objections to the proposed solutions, no argument about the evidence and the Chief Executive thinks we are wonderful, wants to use the process again next time an issue arises in the organisation.'

'Sounds good to me, so what comes next?'

'Well we need to tell everyone what we've found' said Marcus. 'It's important that we get a clear message out about the process that the "Gold Group" went through, what they found and what solutions are being implemented. I just want to sit down with Shelley the union rep first though and brief her, just to make sure there are no likely objections. Once that's done we need to take the various elements of the solution, identify what the quick wins are so we can get on with those straight away, then draw up a longer term plan to cover the rest of the actions that are needed.'

Bob Ainsworth was already on his way out of the office. 'No time like the present, you give Shelley a ring and I'll make a start on working out a plan and sorting out the short term wins and longer term actions.'

When Shelley came into the office, it was clear that the conversation was not going to be easy.

'I hear you are about to cause problems for some of my members'

'On the contrary,' replied Marcus. 'I'm actually going to help them, or most of them anyway.' He went on to explain the process that the Gold Group had gone through, what they had found and the solutions that were proposed. 'That's why I asked you to pop down and see me; I think this is a real win-win. We know that this is the problem, it isn't just guess work and we've got a plan that the "Gold Group" have agreed is suitable for the organisation and offers a sensible long term solution.'

'I can't agree to this. One of the solutions you're wanting to put in place is a new attendance management process for the whole organisation, when the problem is only in a couple of areas.'

'No it's not. Granted the problem is only in four job groups, but they are spread out across the organisation and I'm also trying to look ahead. We've got a problem now that we can fix, but it could happen again and be much more widespread. If we don't take the opportunity to proactively improve our processes now, then we run the risk of a bigger impact on profitability next time and that impacts on the job security of the people you represent.

'Look,' said Shelley, 'I get it but I can't go back to the membership and tell them that I've just let you bring in new arrangements for dealing with sickness, and haven't tried to protect what they already have.'

Marcus smiled. 'I tell you what I'll do, if you stand behind the improvement plan, I'll include you in the team that are planning the implementation. Bob's already gone to break down the actions into those for the short term and those that need a longer lead time.'

'That's all well and good but it will all need proper explanation if the staff are to be convinced. They need to understand that the steps you want to take are truly for the benefit of the majority and not just management taking the opportunity to hit people when they are down.'

'No problem, I'm going to prepare a message for all staff to clarify what has happened so far and what the next steps are. You're welcome to contribute to that and, if it helps, I'm happy to front up a joint roadshow around the various departments and factories to explain what we are doing. At the end of the day, we have the evidence to prove exactly what needs to be done; ultimately, it's difficult to argue against the facts.'

Bob Ainsworth walked back in with an initial draft of the implementation plan. 'Sorry boss I'll come back later.'

'No that's fine, come on in, is that the implementation plan you've got with you? Bring it over here and let's see what Shelley makes of it.'

Later that day, the finalised implementation plan was agreed and a communications strategy was drafted to make sure the message was understood at all levels of the organisation.

'Well I guess that's it now, we just wait to carry out a review 12 months down the line to see if it worked' said Bob. 'Hopefully, we will be looking at improved sickness rates and a healthier organisational bank balance this time next year.'

Marcus just laughed. 'You don't get off as lightly at that. We might have an implementation plan and a communications strategy in place, but we need to make sure we embed a 'new normality' or we risk everything simply remaining unchanged.'

'So how do we do that?'

'Well to begin with, we sell the message again and again and again. Then we check and double check that everyone gets it. That will do to start with.'

Summary – Implement

1. Communicate the outcome.

2. Identify and overcome resistance.

3. Develop an implementation plan.

4. Identify the quick wins and actions for immediate implementation.

5. Complete the plan.

6. Embed the 'new normality'.

CHAPTER 9

Review

Phase 7: Review

Having completed the implementation of your solution, the next task is to carry out a 'REVIEW' and determine whether the solution has been delivered as planned and, if so, whether the outcomes were as intended.

The first element involved in such a 'REVIEW' is to check reality on the ground. One of the best ways to undertake such a task is to carry out an appropriate audit, as this offers a structured and methodical approach that will provide a consistent and defensible set of results. The findings from the audit can then be used to develop an appropriate improvement plan, if one is subsequently found to be required.

There are lots of audit processes available in the marketplace and if you were so inclined you could build your own bespoke version. Another consideration when looking at undertaking an audit is to decide whether you are best placed to undertake the audit yourself or whether it would be best to bring in an independent 'third eye'. With the best will in the world, a person involved in designing and implementing a solution is rarely the best person to make the assessment of whether or not it has been successful. Utilising an independent party from within the organisation or an external consultant to conduct this work will help to add credibility to any eventual outcome and can offer a useful additional perspective on matters.

Whether you undertake a proper audit or simply chose a less structured review the intention is the same, in reality we are seeking answer to three basic questions:

1. Has the new normality been established?

2. Have we achieved what we intended?

3. Were there any unintended consequences that now need to be addressed?

We identified the importance of establishing a new normality as part of 'IMPLEMENT' and discussed some techniques that could be used to help establish it. During 'REVIEW' we are testing whether these steps have been successful. If they have not, there will be an almost inevitable negative impact on the prospects for sustainable improvement in absence, as the organisation is likely to return to its previous state, sooner or later. If you do find this to be the case, it will be necessary to establish precisely what has occurred. By utilising a comprehensive audit tool, the cause and extent of the problem should be readily apparent from the results. If you have opted to follow a less structured approach, it will almost inevitably be necessary to conduct further research to establish this information before moving on to develop an appropriate improvement plan.

Assuming the new normality has been fully embedded, the next question is whether it is delivering what was intended. If you are not seeing the improvement that was expected, there is clearly a need to review why this is the case. In such circumstances, a 'third eye' coming fresh to the problem may spot something that has been missed or can point to a different hypothesis that, if correct, would require an alternative solution to be developed. If this were to occur there would be a need to return to 'PLAN' and call the 'Gold Group' together to develop an investigative strategy necessary to test whether the evidence exists to support this new hypothesis.

The final fundamental question to be addressed as part of 'REVIEW' is whether the solution has led to any unintended consequences. Don't be afraid of this question; it doesn't necessarily point to your identified solution being wrong, it is merely an indication that something else might be happening as a consequence of the solution, which hadn't originally been intended. It may be that the unintended consequence is positive. For example, by tackling poor attendance rates in one area, morale may rise across the organisation as management is seen to be effectively tackling a widely known problem for the benefit of all. If the unintended consequence is negative, then simply consider the link between the two and determine whether there is a need to adjust the original solution or whether the new issue that has surfaced is deserving of assessment in it's own right.

'Real World Approach' – Review

Six months later, Marcus called the "Gold Group" together to review the implementation. This time he also brought along Shelley and the ever-faithful Bob to make sure the feedback loop was complete.

'Okay,' began Marcus, 'three months ago we implemented our solution to the problem of increasing sickness rates. The question is, were our solutions the right ones? Have we seen any improvement?'

'It's still early days yet' replied Shelley. 'We know it takes time to reverse trends in sickness absence and to see that filter through into the figures in a meaningful way. You acknowledged that when we implemented the new arrangements.'

'I do accept that point, but what is the reality on the ground? Has the message got through everywhere? Are we seeing a consistent approach? Are we on track with our implementation plan?'

'It certainly looks that way' said Bob. 'We've definitely stopped the figures getting any worse, but it is taking time to get some of the long term absence cases back to work.'

Marcus wasn't convinced. 'Look, we have to accept that we all have a vested interest in this succeeding, after all it's our plan, but this issue is too important to risk an assessment that is anything but challenging. What I want to do is just check out where we stand by getting someone in from outside the organisation to carry out an independent audit.'

'Oh great, just what we need, some total stranger walking around with a clipboard telling us what we already know' said Penny.

'I take it you don't like consultants?' replied Marcus. 'Look, when Bob did his environmental scan it turned up an on-line assessment tool, that looks at your situation against a range of different factors. We could begin with that and then decide whether we need to bring in any specialist outside help.'

There was a general acceptance around the room that bringing in a 'third eye', either in the form of a consultant or by using a predetermined audit tool had the opportunity to offer important insights. With that agreed, the group agreed to reconvene in a months time to see what further progress had been made.

When the Group reconvened it was Fred the Marketing Manager who started the conversation. 'Okay, what does your audit tell us?'

'I don't quite know how to put this,' Marcus said. 'We've completed the audit and then run the results against a database the consultants use.'

'And? What did we miss?' demanded Penny. 'I knew we should have stopped whilst we were winning and not wasted our money on consultants.'

'That's where you're wrong Penny' said Marcus with a beaming smile on his face. 'The audit gave us a clean bill of health. The sickness figures are still not as good as I would like, but they continue to go down slowly and all of the evidence points to a sustained improvement that will become more evident over the coming months. The audit confirmed that we have buy-in for our processes across the organisation, so we have achieved what we set out to do with the improvement plan, we have established a new normality.'

Summary – Review

1. Review the implementation.

2. Check reality on the ground.

3. Carry out an audit.

4. Bring in a 'third eye'.

5. Has a 'new normality' been established?

6. Have the changes achieved what was intended?

7. Were there any unintended consequences that now need to be addressed?

CHAPTER 10

Protect

Phase 8: Protect

There is one final phase left to complete the process and that is 'PROTECT'. If you wonder whether this is really worth the effort, just ask yourself would the organisation welcome dealing with the same type of problem all over again? Whilst the previous steps minimises the risk of the exact same issue repeating itself, 'PROTECT' provides 'target hardening' thus helping to avoid the issue morphing and recurring in a different guise.

If we are going to effectively 'PROTECT', then the first thing that is required is to learn lessons from the past. This can be harder to achieve than one would think, particularly if the organisation has a 'blame culture'. It is almost inevitable in that situation that individuals would wish to present themselves and their team in the best possible light and will thus often seek to hide from any difficulties and attempt to deflect criticism that they perceive is heading their way. What is particularly problematic is that this can be a very subtle process, with people proactively taking very early defensive steps to ensure they don't come into focus. Whilst a thorough investigative process helps, it needs to be recognised that developing an open, trusting and mutually supportive culture in an organisation is the best way to ensure you become a learning organisation and gain the full benefit from any lessons that arise.

The other key feature that is required, if you wish to effectively 'PROTECT', is to reinforce a mind-set of continuous development and improvement. If people are always looking for improvement, then they are far more likely to be accepting of opportunities to do things differently. This is particularly the case when the evidence exists to demonstrate the value of making the change and this should readily flow from the Investig8™ process.

But what if you don't have an open, trusting and mutually supportive culture? What if all of the managers in all of the areas of your organisation are focused on blame rather than continuous development and improvement? What if you have an adversarial relationship with staff representatives? Well, in the real world, that is where most of us are to a greater or lesser extent; even where there is a largely positive culture most of the time, there will be occasions where some individuals will be off-side. Similarly, even where there is an on-going organisational focus on improvement some will fear certain aspects of change and at that point will prefer to take the road of the Luddite and defend what they know rather than take a chance on something new. Faced with this reality, the crucial final part of the jigsaw is an effective performance framework that offers the opportunity for on-going insightful monitoring.

The problem with most performance frameworks is that they fail to strike the right balance. Often they are focused purely on data that is presented in a manner that is over simplified or over complicated. How many times have you wished for greater granularity of detail on a particular issue only to then find yourself a few months down the line overwhelmed with masses of data that is preventing you from seeing the true nature of the problem? The truth is that each situation differs and, as a result, so do your requirements; they can change depending on the issue to be dealt with or they can change depending on the specific role you have. The solution is to develop a data set that operates at different levels, allowing you to see the big picture, but then drill into the detail if that becomes necessary. For example, the first thing you will probably want to know is the overall rate of absence. If the rate is low, that may be enough for a Chief Executive. If the rate is high, or you are in a strategic human resources role then you may want more detail, such as:

What are the rates of absence at each main site?

What are the rates of absence for each major employment group?

What are the main causes of absence?

... and so the list goes on. If I am responsible for absence management as a line manager or specialist support officer I will want more detail, but only that which is specific to my area. The problem, therefore, becomes how to display such an array of information in a meaningful way. Sound familiar? This is just the sort of issue that we discussed in Phase 2 - 'COLLECT INTELLIGENCE' and there is a good reason for that. The information that makes good intelligence is also the information that helps to 'PROTECT' the organisation, its staff and its customer from future problems arising, provided it forms part of a responsive and comprehensive on-going monitoring process.

The same point is relevant to environmental scans. These also shows up as a key element of 'COLLECT INTELLIGENCE' and provide useful data about the latest developments, where 'best practice' has been found, what legislative changes are coming, what recent case law is saying, all of which are vital pieces of information to help with the on-going protection of the organisation. The environmental scan might merely provide information of note, or it might provide a useful insight that prompts a complete change of approach. As previously highlighted, such scans can sound daunting and time consuming, but once you have identified the sources to feed your environmental scan they tend to remain consistent and it is purely a question of revisiting those sources and pulling together the information and creating one single briefing document.

The next part of an effective protection regime is a risk assessment framework. Again, this isn't a complex task, but it is a vital one. As we demonstrated in 'COLLECT INTELLIGENCE' this need only consist of a simple assessment of likelihood and impact, but will provide you with sufficient information to score each issue and enable you to determine the main threats and risks that need to be dealt with.

The final element of a protection framework is the action plan. This we haven't covered before, but is in essence a summary of all the work that is due to be progressed in relation to issue at hand - in this case absence management. The action plan should be prioritised to ensure there is appropriate focus on delivery of the most important tasks; this can be achieved by a basic high/medium/low rating system. Each action should have a clearly identified outcome, a named person who is responsible for delivery and a due delivery date. The action plan should be regularly updated and progress recorded against each action. If you are operating the plan properly, it should bring together all of the different elements of the protection framework. If your data sets point to an issue, then dealing with that issue would feature as an action. If your environmental scan points to a new piece of 'best practice' it would become an action to review and if relevant implement it. Similarly, if your risk matrix has identified certain high risks, then the plan for how to reduce those risks will also feature as actions.

I appreciate that developing such a framework can appear daunting but it needn't be. There are specialists available who can help with the design and on-line solutions do exist. Equally, having now read this book, there is nothing to stop you developing your own framework based on the knowledge you have now gained.

There is one additional element to the protection framework, but one that doesn't need to be updated as regularly, so it effectively sits slightly apart from the other elements and that is the audit process. We covered audits as part of 'REVIEW' in the previous chapter so there is no need to go into the detail again here; suffice to say that an annual audit can provide a valuable reality check of what is happening on the ground. Remember, you can have the best processes in the world, but if nobody is following them or they are misunderstood, then they are effectively useless. An annual audit ensures that you have an awareness of what is actually going on and helps in the development of pre-emptive action to prevent problems from occurring.

'Real World Approach' – Protect

Marcus headed for the Chief Executive's office.

'I can't tell you how pleased I am,' began Helen Starling. 'Sickness rates are beginning to fall, the union is on board with the changes we have made and looking at that audit that was carried out, it appears that there is full awareness of the new arrangements and a willingness to adopt them across all functions.'

'I'm glad you're pleased, but that isn't the end. We need to make sure that we learn our lessons from what went wrong before and take steps to ensure it doesn't happen again.'

Helen rolled her eyes. 'You're never satisfied are you. Look I'm pleased with what has been achieved but that's enough, it's time to move on, sickness isn't a problem anymore. The changes you introduced are working, we've completed an audit that proves it, what more could we possibly need to do?'

Marcus considered his position for a moment. Contradicting the Chief Executive was not a great career move, but neither was simply rolling over when you are truly committed to something and knew it would make a lasting difference. Weighing up the options he calculated he had enough brownie points in the bag to push the issue. 'Can I be brutally honest with you?'

'I would hope you always are.' Helen looked far from pleased, but just as Marcus was beginning to think better of it she pushed the intercom button on her desk and called out to her PA. 'Can you cancel my 10:30 and bring in some coffee, I think I'm going to need it.'

'Right Marcus, you have my undivided attention, give me your honest assessment.'

'Can I take you back to our original conversation about sickness, when I asked what your perception of the problem was?'

'Yes, what of it? It was just a situation that needed gripping and I was right, you've gripped it now and we don't have a problem.'

Marcus pressed on undeterred. 'Well there was an issue when you last gripped sickness. You found a problem with back pain in a factory and pushed for it to be addressed.'

'I repeat, what of it? It was a big issue at the time, I focused on it and the problem went away.'

'It didn't, it just morphed into another problem. Don't get me wrong your input really helped reduce sickness, but only for a short time. Everyone knew you were focused on absence and back pain in particular and for a period of time attendance went up.'

Helen fought back. 'Look here Marcus, I've kept an eye on the data and my intervention did more than you claim. Back pain no longer features in our top causes of absence, so my input worked long term. I will accept that it's started to increase in recent months, but that just means it's time for me to push the issue again.'

Marcus paused before responding. 'I'm sorry to tell you this, but your input did nothing to improve back pain. All that happened was that the worst performing departments simply coded the absence to something else. The reason it's going up now is that I've spoken to those departments to let them know I'm aware of the issue and asked them to correct the situation. If you go out and push the issue of back pain, we will just repeat the earlier mistake and that's the point really.'

Helen Starling looked shocked. 'Surely, I'm not that much of a tyrant? I can't believe people have done that. Who is responsible for this?'

'I don't think anyone is responsible, it was just an unintended consequence of the intervention. What I'm pushing for now is a prevention strategy that will protect the organisation into the future and ensure that something like that doesn't happen again. We've already taken some steps to check this out by running the audit process but at the moment that's seen as a one-off. What I'd like to do is run something similar every year or so, just to make sure that we are still focused on all of the things we should be doing and checking that the message is still out there. It wouldn't cost much, we can use an on-line tool, so given the potential savings I think it's a no brainer.'

'Okay, that's not a problem, we can do that. What else are you wanting to do?'

'I want to alter the reporting framework for the sickness data. I want to look at the information in a more structured way that gives you the high level strategic data you need to see, I would then have more detail and Bob and the team would be working with a full set of statistics. We've already got the data so it's just about how it's presented and working out what are the most important things to focus on, so again the cost is minimal and the detail is there if we want to drill down at any point'

'Is that it?'

'Pretty much. We will use the data as early warning signs and link this to a regularly updated environmental scan to ensure we are picking up on best practice from elsewhere and keeping abreast of the latest developments. We can link the key bits of information they provide into a risk matrix and that will ensure that we continue to focus on the areas of greatest threat or greatest benefit and that will ensure we continually develop our processes and "target harden'" by taking proactive action where necessary.'

Marcus knew he had won the day, but Helen still needed convincing that this wasn't going to be a bureaucratic nightmare.

'I don't need any extra staff for any of this,' said Marcus. 'If anything, this makes life easier, it's just about putting existing information into a clear reporting structure that brings key data together in one place, with key developments and key risks. We just need to make sure that this then drives our work programme, which we can check by completing regular audits. It's simple really.'

'Okay you've got my backing. Thanks Marcus .... I always knew it was a good idea to recruit a good quality HR lead to the organisation and bring them into the top team. No one can say that you're just providing back office support, this is really impacting on the operations of the organisation and improving the balance sheet.'

Summary – Protect

1. Learn the lessons.

2. Target harden.

3. Establish a 'develop and improve' organisational mind-set.

4. Embed a performance framework for on-going monitoring.

CHAPTER 11

Summary

SUMMARY

I hope you have found this book of interest. More than anything I trust that the layout has helped you gain some new learning and insights than can help you in your 'real world', even if you chose not to adopt the whole model. My intention in writing this book was not to provide an in-depth theoretical text book; rather, I wanted to introduce you to a practical approach that offers the opportunity to solve one of those perennial problems faced by organisations around the world, namely how best to manage absence.

In the hurly burly world faced by modern day organisations, there is a real temptation to go for the quick fix. I hope what this book proves is that a properly structured approach, built around a set of sound investigative principles, need take no more time than the quick fix. It never ceases to amaze me when I talk to people from other organisations how many look on in awe when you explain such an approach. Time after time people come forward and tell me how great it must be to have the resources to do something as thorough as this. When I explain how little time is actually required and that the resource necessary pays for itself many times over, they struggle to comprehend how this could be so. But it is!

The Invesitg8™ process is not complex. If you have a problem in your organisation I would strongly recommend that you try it in its entirely at least once, it works!! It will stop you chasing your tail and implementing solutions that are not properly thought through or are just plain wrong. By adopting the evidenced based approach that lies behind Investig8™ you will save both time and money.

If a problem has yet to occur, then the data and audit requirements that I recommend in the 'PROTECT' phase will help to ensure that it never does. If you look around your organisation the vast majority of the data you need is already available, the problem is how that data is currently being used. All too often it is presented in incomprehensible tables that need time and a degree in statistics to understand properly, or you receive too little data to truly understand what is happening. What I am recommending is a reporting mechanism that allows you to see the big picture, but then offers the opportunity to focus on those issues that are of greatest importance. In terms of the environmental scans, risk matrices, action plans and audits, these are not complicated to set up and once in place are easy to keep updated.

For those who have just focused on the bullet point summaries, I do appreciate the time pressures that caused you to follow that route, and am grateful that this has at least prevented the book from becoming another item of shelf decoration. If you have taken this path and found yourself struggling to understand any of the concepts just delve into the relevant chapter; they are designed to be self-standing so the additional effort required to fully grasp the concepts should be minimal.

Finally, thank you for taking the time to read this book. If you would like any further help or guidance on applying the Invesitg8™ model or have any specific queries in relation to the theory or its application in your organisation please feel free to contact me at realworldapproach@gmail.com.

Made in the USA
Charleston, SC
05 July 2013